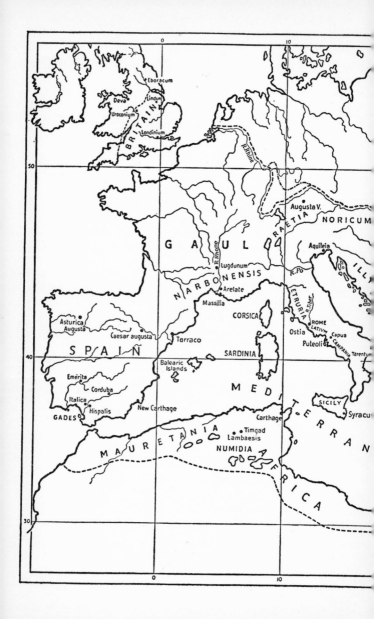

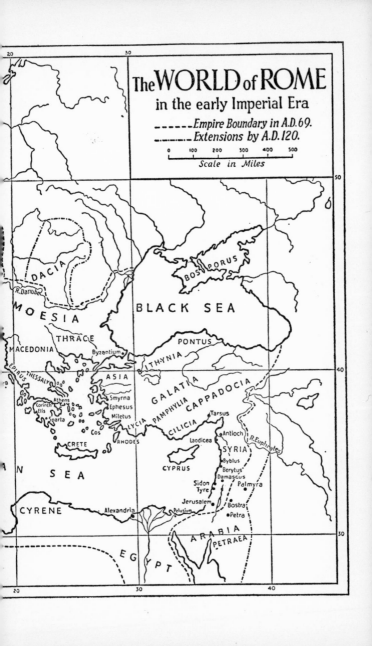

The WORLD of ROME
in the early Imperial Era

- - - - - Empire Boundary in A.D. 69.
- ·—·—· Extensions by A.D. 120.

0   100   200   300   400   500
Scale in Miles

DACIA

R.Danube

MOESIA

THRACE

MACEDONIA

EPIRUS

THESSALY

Corinth
Elis
Athens
Sparta

Byzantium

BLACK SEA

BOSPORUS

PONTUS

BITHYNIA

ASIA

GALATIA

PAMPHYLIA

Smyrna
Ephesus
Miletus

Cos

LYCIA

RHODES

CRETE

CAPPADOCIA

Tarsus

CILICIA

Antioch

R.Euphrates

Laodicea

CYPRUS

SYRIA

Byblus
Berytus

Sidon
Tyre

Damascus

Palmyra

Jerusalem

N   SEA

CYRENE

Alexandria

Pelusium

Bostra

Petra

ARABIA

PETRAEA

EGYPT

THE TEACH YOURSELF BOOKS
EDITED BY LEONARD CUTTS

ARCHAEOLOGY OF
THE NEW TESTAMENT

THE TEACH YOURSELF BOOKS

ARCHAEOLOGY
of the

NEW TESTAMENT

Professor R. K. HARRISON, Ph.D.
Wycliffe College, University of Toronto

THE ENGLISH UNIVERSITIES PRESS LTD.
102 NEWGATE STREET
LONDON · EC1

First printed 1964

Copyright © 1964
The English Universities Press Ltd.

PRINTED AND BOUND IN ENGLAND
FOR THE ENGLISH UNIVERSITIES PRESS LTD BY
HAZELL WATSON AND VINEY LTD
AYLESBURY BUCKS

PREFACE

THE present volume completes a triad of works dealing with the general subject of Biblical archaeology in the *Teach Yourself* series, its precursors being *The Dead Sea Scrolls* and *Archaeology of the Old Testament*. Like them it has been written with the general reader in mind, but some annotation has been provided in the hope that the book may be of use to more advanced students of the subject.

I wish to acknowledge the kindness of the Editor of *The Biblical Archaeologist* for permitting me to quote copyright material from that Journal. I am also particularly grateful to Messrs. E. J. Brill of Leiden, who graciously granted me permission to use several quotations from *The Gospel According to Thomas* (1959), translated by A. Guillamont, H-Ch. Puech, G. Quispel, W. Till and Yassah 'Abd Al Masiḥ. It is a pleasure also to acknowledge the kindly interest and counsel of Professor E. M. Blaiklock, of the University of Auckland, New Zealand. Finally my thanks are due to Mrs. H. Bohne, Assistant Librarian of Wycliffe College, Toronto, for her invaluable assistance with source materials, and to my colleague the Rev. Norman Green, Field Secretary of Wycliffe College, for expert help with much of the photographic material in this book.

Wycliffe College,
  University of Toronto

R. K. HARRISON

CONTENTS

PLATES

The illustrations are included as one section between
pages 82 and 83 .

The endpapers show The World of Rome in The
Early Imperial Era

ABBREVIATIONS

1QS	*The Community Rule* or *Manual of Discipline.*
CDC	*The Code of the Cairo Damascene Covenanters.*
1QISa	St. Mark's Monastery Isaiah Scroll.
1QISb	Hebrew University's Isaiah Scroll.
1QH	The Thanksgiving Hymns.
1QM	The Military Scroll.
1QpHab	The Qumran Habakkuk Commentary.
A.V.	The Authorised (King James) Version (1611).
R.V.	The Revised Version (1881).
R.S.V.	The Revised Standard Version (1952).
N.E.B.	The New English Bible, New Testament (1961).
LXX	The Septuagint (Greek) Old Testament.
AJ	Flavius Josephus, *The Antiquities of the Jews* (Whiston ed., 1829).
AJA	*American Journal of Archaeology.*
AP	W. F. Albright, *The Archaeology of Palestine* (1949).
ARE	J. H. Breasted, *Ancient Records of Egypt* (1906–07). 5 vols.
BA	*The Biblical Archaeologist.*
BASOR	*Bulletin of the American Schools of Oriental Research.*
BRD	W. M. Ramsay, *The Bearing of Recent Discovery on the Trustworthiness of the New Testament* (1914).
CALQ	F. M. Cross, *The Ancient Library of Qumran* (1961).
DSSET	T. H. Gaster, *The Dead Sea Scriptures in English Translation* (1956).

ET	*The Expository Times.*
GAT	A. Guillaumont, H-Ch. Puech, G. Quispel, W. Till and Yassah 'Abd Al Masiḥ (Transl.), *The Gospel According to Thomas* (1959).
JBL	*Journal of Biblical Literature and Exegesis.*
JEA	*Journal of Egyptian Archaeology.*
JJS	*Journal of Jewish Studies.*
JQR	*Jewish Quarterly Review.* New Series.
JTS	*Journal of Theological Studies.*
KBA	E. G. Kraeling, *Bible Atlas* (1956).
LAP	J. Finegan, *Light From the Ancient Past* (1946).
LSCA	W. M. Ramsay, *The Letters to the Seven Churches of Asia* (1904).
MM	J. H. Moulton and G. Milligan, *The Vocabulary of the Greek Testament* (1949).
NAD	C. M. Coburn, *The New Archaeological Discoveries* (1917).
NT	*Novum Testamentum.*
NTS	*New Testament Studies.*
NTRC	W. M. Ramsay, *St. Paul the Traveller and the Roman Citizen* (1897).
RB	*Revue Biblique.*
SNT	K. Stendahl (Ed.), *The Scrolls and the New Testament* (1957).
VT	*Vetus Testamentum.*
WBA	G. E. Wright, *Biblical Archaeology* (1957).
WHAB	G. E. Wright and F. V. Filson, *The Westminster Historical Atlas to the Bible* (1957).
WJ	Flavius Josephus, *The Wars of the Jews* (Whiston ed., 1829).
WMTS	M. Burrows, *What Mean These Stones?* (1941).

Chapter I

SOURCES FOR STUDY

BECAUSE the spectacular discoveries which initiated the era of Biblical archaeology were concerned primarily with the Old Testament, it has been too readily assumed in some quarters that the spade has thrown little if any light upon the pages of the New Testament. In point of fact the modern excavator has uncovered impressive amounts of material constituting a valuable array of evidence in support of the history, religion, sociology and topography of the early Christian period as represented in the New Testament. As is the case also with the Old Testament, the work of the archaeologist has done much to modify earlier radical theories about the New Testament, and to confirm the general witness of the early Church to the authentic nature of primitive Christianity.

However, the most important discoveries in this area have seldom been attended by such striking circumstances as those surrounding the unearthing of the winged human-headed lions at Nineveh by A. H. Layard, which when excavated provoked from the Arab chief at Mosul the sober comment:

"This is not the work of man's hands, but of those infidel giants of whom the Prophet (peace be with him) has said that they were higher than the tallest date tree. This is one of the idols which Noah (peace be with him) cursed before the flood."[1]

Nor is there the same sense of antiquity in the New Testament field as that connected, for example, with the excavation of the Royal Tombs at Ur by Woolley,[2] the recovery of ancient cultures at Mari[3] and Nuzu[4], the finding of the Tell el-Amarna tablets[5] and many other dramatic examples of Old Testament archaeological activity.

Although there are occasions of great moment, such as that which occurred on January 12th, 1897, when Hunt recognised the Greek word *karphos* on a scrap of Egyptian papyrus and realised that he was holding in his hand a short series of the sayings of Christ almost contemporary with the Gospel writings,[6] the work of the New Testament archaeologist has been concerned primarily with the commoner objects of day to day life at the beginning of the Christian era.[7] In this connection fragments of pottery and glass, pieces of jewelry, discarded metal objects, broken weapons and the like are of great importance in piecing together the life of the people. Many of the most significant discoveries resulting from excavations have been proved to consist of written records of one sort or another, inscribed on stone, alabaster, papyrus, leather or broken pottery, and have been recovered from Egyptian mummies, Judaean caves, ruined buildings and rubbish heaps. Pottery in particular had been used for centuries as a cheap and convenient medium for written communications, and such inscribed ostraca as have been recovered from Palestine in the New Testament period have included letters, receipts, lists, records and other written material.

Of considerable importance for the archaeologists are deposits of coins, both for dating the levels at which they occur and for the historic material which they contain. The oldest coins discovered up to the present were supposed to have been minted at Sardis, capital of Lydia, during the seventh century B.C. Assyrian loan and payment records dated between 676 and 671 B.C. seem to indicate the use of coined shekels stamped with the head of Ishtar, but none of them has been recovered as yet.[8] Gold Persian darics were brought to Palestine in 536 B.C. by the Jews who were returning from captivity,[9] and coins from the third century B.C. and later have been uncovered at almost all occupational levels in Palestinian excavations.

That they are of considerable material aid in determining sequences and dates can be illustrated from the excavations at Qumran,[10] where over seven hundred and fifty coins were recovered in or near the community settlement. The coins began with the reign of John Hyrcanus (135–104 B.C.) at level I in the Hasmonean period, and continued without interruption to the time of Mattathias (40–37 B.C.), the last of the Hasmoneans. Only one coin was recovered from the period of Herod the Great (37–4 B.C.), whereas a number were dated in the reign of his son and successor Herod Archelaus (4 B.C.–A.D. 6). Other coins came from the period of the Roman procurators of Judaea under Augustus (A.D. 6–14), Tiberius (A.D. 14–37), Claudius (A.D. 44–54) and Nero (A.D. 54–66). Twenty-three coins of Herod Agrippa I (A.D. 37–44) were also uncovered, furnishing a continuous historical record to the beginning of the First Jewish Revolt (A.D. 66–70), while others were dated after the fall of Jerusalem in A.D. 70. About a dozen coins came from the time of the Second Jewish Revolt (A.D. 132–5).

In 63 B.C. Pompey had introduced Roman coinage into Palestine, making for a wide variety of Greek and Roman currency.[11] The Greek coins mentioned in the Gospels included the silver *drachma*,[12] the *didrachma*,[13] and the *tetradrachm*.[14] The *talent*[15] and the silver *mina* or "pound"[16] were really weights of silver rather than actual coinage. The Roman *denarius* or "penny" was common currency in the early Christian period,[17] as were the bronze "farthing" or *quadrans*,[18] the *as* or *assarion*[19] and

the very small bronze "mite" or *lepton*.[20] The silver
Roman coins formed the principal monetary standard of
Judaea in the days of Christ, and it was the silver
denarius of Tiberius Caesar which Jesus held in His hand
when the Herodians sought to trap Him.[21]

The coins minted by Herod the Great were the first
to replace the Hebrew inscriptions with Greek forms, but
avoided the use of pagan symbols in deference to Jewish
religious strictures regarding graven images. Herod
Agrippa I, however, had no such scruples, frequently
representing the Imperial head on the obverse of the
coin, while on the reverse were depicted pagan temples,
Greek goddesses and the like, along with neutral symbols
which included ears of barley and palm trees.

The tiny *lepton* was first minted during the Maccabean
period, and has been recovered in large quantities from
many sites. While its small size made legible stamping
difficult, it is possible nevertheless to determine typical
patterns and to assign the coins to the reigns of Herod the
Great, Herod Archelaus, the Procurator Valerius and the
Procurator Pilate. The *lepton* was worth about one four-
hundredth part of a shekel.[22]

Valuable philological and historical information has
been furnished for the archaeologist by the wide variety
of inscriptions in Palestine. These range from the well-
executed lead-lined specimens occurring in the early
Roman period to the more informal *graffiti*, which consisted of writing scratched on the surface of a rock or wall
without being too deeply engraved. On other occasions
inscriptions occurred in painted form on the inside of
tombs, following ancient Egyptian practices, or marked
in carbon on a coffin or a wall. This material is of major
importance in that it furnishes the names of people and
places, and frequently supplies detailed information
concerning customs, laws and events which would otherwise be unknown.

In this connection inscriptions from public buildings are normally of great interest to the archaeologist. Thus the oldest trace of a synagogue in Palestine is contained in an inscription found by Raymond Weill[23] in the excavations at the southern end of the mound Ophel in Jerusalem, and published in 1920. The inscription referred to the building of a synagogue as follows:

"Theodotus son of Vettenus priest and synagogue-president, son of a synagogue-president, has built the synagogue for the reading of the Law and the teaching of the commandments and (he has built) the hostelry and the chambers and the cisterns of water in order to provide lodgings for those from abroad who need them —(the synagogue) which his fathers and the elders and Simonides had founded."[24]

This inscription would indicate that either Theodotus or his ancestor must have been a freedman from Italy, since the patronymic *gens Vettena* was that of a well-known Roman family. There may well be good reason for connecting this synagogue with that of the Libertines (Freedmen), which constituted the strongest support for Jewish orthodoxy in its contention with Stephen.[25] This synagogue was probably erected when Christ was living in Nazareth.

Other interesting contemporary inscriptions have been recovered from tiles and drains in the ruins of buildings. Some of these artefacts bore the name of the maker,[26] or the title of the Imperial legion responsible for the construction of the building. The tenth Roman legion, which occupied Palestine for a lengthy period, left behind a good many of these inscriptions, which frequently appeared in Latin on tiles as LEG. X. FRE or LEG. X. F.[27] One inscription from Jerusalem spoke of a soldier who had died on garrison duty in Palestine, and read as follows:

D M L MAGNIUS FELIX, MIL LEG X FRET,
B TRIB MIL ANN XVIII VIX XXXIX.[28]

Other material of considerable importance for studying the origins of Christianity has been recovered from tombs and graves of the Roman period. Some of these repositories of the dead were architectural monuments,[29] one of which was known as the "Tombs of the Kings".[30] It was in fact the burial chamber of Queen Helena of Adiabene and her family. She was converted to Judaism about A.D. 46, and went to live in Jerusalem some twenty years before the Jewish revolt of A.D. 66–70. Her sarcophagus was recovered when the mausoleum was excavated by F. de Saulcy in 1863, and a bilingual Hebrew and Syriac inscription from it is now in the Louvre in Paris.[31] Another rock-cut tomb in the Hinnom Valley showed early Roman architectural influences, and can be assigned to a period prior to A.D. 70.

Many of the larger tombs contained chambers lined with shelves, on which were placed small ossuaries or stone caskets containing human bones. When room was needed for new burials it was the custom of the Jews to collect the bones from the decomposed remains of earlier interments and place them in ossuaries.[32] These containers were normally made of limestone, and were often decorated with mosaic work and a variety of inlays. The names of the deceased were invariably carved upon the ossuaries in Hebrew, Aramaic or Greek,[33] and these inscriptions have contributed materially to an understanding of contemporary family and social organisation. Such names as Jesus (Jeshua), son of Joseph, Simon or Simeon, Judas, Ananias, Saphira, Elizabeth and many others indicate that the names in the New Testament were in fact the common names of the day. In 1931 an un-

usually interesting ossuary inscription was discovered in
the Russian museum on the Mount of Olives. Originally
it had been associated with an ancient burial site, but
had at some subsequent time been removed from the
grave. It read:

"Hither were brought the bones of Uzziah, king of
Judah—do not open."[34]

The inscription was neatly carved on a slab of stone in the
Aramaic script of the time of Christ, which would suggest that when repairs or excavations were being undertaken in Jerusalem during the first centuries B.C. or
A.D., the original tomb of the great king had been en-
countered and his bones removed to another location.

There appear to be good reasons for assuming that
some of the earliest evidences of Christianity have been
discovered among the ossuaries from the cemeteries
around Jerusalem. In 1945 E. L. Sukenik excavated a
tomb discovered in the Jerusalem suburb of Talpioth,[35]
and on removing some of the ossuaries he observed that
five of them were inscribed. Three of the inscriptions
were in Aramaic and contained the names Simon
Barsaba, Miriam daughter of Simeon, and Mat'.[36] The
other two caskets bore Greek inscriptions which proved
difficult to decipher, although the name of Jesus appeared clearly on each, followed in one case by the word
Iou and in the other by *Aloth*.[37] In addition, one of the
containers was marked with crosses drawn in charcoal.
Sukenik suggested that the group of three ossuaries
constituted the remains of a Christian family, and
postulated an identification with "Joseph called Barsabas",[38] a prominent member of the early Christian
Church. There may also be a connection with "Judas
named Barsabas",[39] who was one of the disciples sent
to Antioch with Paul and Barnabas at the conclusion of

the Council of Jerusalem. While precise identification is
impossible at the present, there can be no question as to
the importance of these and similar remains for the study
of Christian origins.

But by far the commonest inscribed material in Palestine at the commencement of the Christian era was
papyrus,[40] a sedge which still grows plentifully in parts
of the Sudan.[41] Originally adopted as a nome-emblem in
Lower Egypt to match the lotus of Upper Egypt, the
papyrus plant was as renowned religiously and artistic-
ally[42] as it was deemed useful for a wide variety of purposes in everyday life. Perhaps the most significant of the
latter was the utilising of the tough pellicles of the stem
to produce the first practicable and inexpensive writing
material known to man.

While a statuette of an ancient Egyptian scribe holding
a roll of papyrus has been recovered from the period of
the Third Dynasty (*c.* 2700 B.C.),[43] the oldest specimen
of an actual papyrus manuscript is dated in the Fifth
Dynasty (*c.* 2300 B.C.).[44] During the successive centuries
papyrus came into increasing use, and later spread into
other lands[45] where the climate was conducive to its
preservation. As described by Pliny,[46] papyrus was pre-
pared by being split into thin strips which were then
laid horizontally and vertically, moistened with the
muddy water of the Nile, and when dry rubbed smooth
by means of a flat stone. Several such sheets were glued
together side by side to form one continuous roll measuring on the average about nine inches by up to fifteen
feet.[47] The papyrus was normally inscribed on the *recto*
side, where the fibres ran horizontally,[48] in a series of
columns some two or three inches wide. Scribes used
pens made from a thoroughly dry reed stalk[49] and wrote
in ink,[50] of which there were two kinds.[51]

The usual form of a book in the first century A.D. was
the papyrus roll or *biblion*,[52] which in the plural, *biblia*,[53]

was used by the early Christians in connection with the books of the New Testament. When the limitations of the roll for practical purposes became apparent, it was superceded by the codex[54] in which the separate sheets of a manuscript were fastened together as in the modern book. If the codex was not actually a Christian invention it was certainly in use among the Christians of the second century A.D.[55] The earliest fragment of a New Testament papyrus codex consists of a small portion of the Fourth Gospel, measuring about three and a half inches by two and a quarter inches. It had been acquired by B. P. Grenfell with some other Egyptian papyri in 1920, and was discovered fifteen years later in the John Rylands Library archives in Manchester.[56] On palaeographic grounds it is dated in the first half of the second century A.D.

The oldest copy of the Pauline letters recovered to date is a codex included in a group of papyrus manuscripts which were discovered by some Egyptian peasants and marketed in 1931. Portions of this collection were acquired by the University of Michigan[57] and certain other individuals, but the bulk of it was purchased by A. Chester Beatty, after whom the Pauline codex is commonly named.[58] The entire group of papyri, consisting of eleven codices which included portions of the Old Testament and certain non-canonical writings, has been dated between the second and fourth centuries A.D., and may have constituted the library of some Christian church or community. On palaeographic and other grounds the papyrus copy of the Pauline epistles has been assigned to *c*. A.D. 200[59]. This codex is thus only about one hundred and fifty years removed from the time when the majority of the letters of Paul were written.

Leather had been used for some centuries prior to this time as writing material,[60] and was particularly valuable in countries where the climate was unfavourable to the

preservation of papyrus. By about the fourth century
A.D. it superceded papyrus in the form of parchment or
vellum,[61] and persisted for some purposes of literary
communication long after the invention of paper and
printing.

In the early Christian period manuscripts were written
without any punctuation or breaks between words.
Gradually divisions appeared in the text, followed by
headings and subscriptions. The sacred names were
commonly abbreviated, as were such words as *man*[62] and
cross.[63] These factors presented little difficulty to the
skilled reader, but raised many possibilities of confusion
and error when the New Testament manuscripts began
to be copied out for wide circulation. In the early
Christian era it was customary for literary productions
to be written in a formal bookhand script similar to
capital letters, and known as "uncial". The great Codex
Sinaiticus, which was discovered by Constantine Tischendorf in the Monastery of St. Catherine on Mount
Sinai[64] and found to consist of the entire Bible along with
some non-canonical writings, was written in an elegant
capital script, as was also the Codex Vaticanus[65] and
many other New Testament codices made between the
fourth and ninth centuries A.D.

Because uncial script involved a good deal of time and
effort, a non-literary or "cursive" script also grew up in
the Roman period. As adapted to the requirements of
Biblical writings it grew into a smaller script than the
uncial and had differently shaped letters, many of which
could be written in connected form without lifting the
pen from the papyrus sheet. This kind of hand became
known as "minuscule", and about the ninth century
A.D. began to supercede uncial script. The vast majority
of New Testament manuscripts and fragments are written in minuscule.[66]

These practices throw some light on certain references

in the Pauline letters, which, being non-literary in
character, would almost certainly have been written
by a scribe in cursive script.[67] Paul occasionally added a
closing sentence or two in his own handwriting,[68]
which he himself described in Galatians as being written
with "large letters".[69] This may be taken to mean that
by comparison with the practised, flowing script of the
amanuensis, Paul's own writing was relatively stiff and
angular in character. From this it will be clear that the
differing styles of writing exhibited by New Testament
manuscripts are a valuable aid in establishing the
approximate date of the documents themselves.

The importance of papyrus as the "instrument of so
great a deliverance"[70] in the field of New Testament
studies was becoming apparent in 1890, when Flinders
Petrie excavated a Ptolemaic cemetery in the Egyptian
Fayyum and found large quantities of papyrus manuscripts which had been stuffed inside coffins. Grenfell,
Hunt and Hogarth continued work in that locality,[71] and
at Tebtunis excavated a crocodile cemetery[72] which to
their amazement disclosed that the sacred animals had
been stuffed with papyrus rolls before being interred.
Early in 1897 came the celebrated discovery of the third
century A.D. *Oxyrhynchus Sayings of Jesus*, to be followed
in 1903 by a second fragment containing other words of
Christ,[73] and subsequently by countless other papyri
dealing with a vast range of topics common to everyday
life. Their importance can be gathered from the remarks
of Moulton, who observed that the lost Classical treatises
and the sayings of Christ recovered at the beginning of
the century

"... must yield in importance to the spoil which has
been gathered from the wills, official reports, private
letters, petitions, accounts, and other trivial survivals
from the rubbish heaps of antiquity."[74]

The character of these documents can be illustrated by a "letter of commendation"[75] written by a certain Theon to his brother, the royal scribe of the district:

"Theon to Heraclides his brother, many greetings and wishes for good health. Hermophilus the bearer of this letter is (the friend or relative) of . . . erius, and asked me to write to you. Hermophilus declares that he has business at Kerkemounis. Please therefore further him in this matter, as is just. For the rest take care of yourself that you may remain in good health. Goodbye. The third year of Tiberius Caesar Augustus, Phaophi 3.

On the *verso* the address was as follows:

"To Heraclides, basilicogrammateus of the Oxyrhynchite and Cynopolite nomes."[76]

A letter written by a female slave of the second century A.D. to her sick master showed genuine sympathy for the sufferer:

"Tays to the lord Apollonius, many greetings. Above all I greet you master, and am praying always for your health. I was distressed, lord, in no small measure to hear that you were sick; but thanks be to all the gods that they are keeping you from all harm. I beseech you, lord, if you think it right, to send to us; if not we die, because we do not see you daily.[77] Would that we . . . could come and pay our reverence to you. For we are distressed . . . Goodbye, lord, . . . All is going well with us. Epeiph. 24."[78]

Another document from the same period was written by a prodigal son to his mother:

"Antonis Longus to Nilus his mother many greetings.
Continually I pray for your health. Supplication on
your behalf I direct each day to the Lord Serapis.[79]
I wish you to know that I had no hope that you would
come up to the metropolis. On this account neither
did I enter into the city. But I was ashamed to come
to Karanis,[80] because I am going about in rags. I
write to you that I am naked. I beseech you, mother,
be reconciled to me. But I know what I have brought
upon myself. Punished I have been every way. I
know that I have sinned . . ."[81]

Many other similar documents dealing with almost
every aspect of everyday affairs could be cited[82] to
demonstrate the remarkably modern life of the ancient
Mediterranean world. But perhaps the most important
discovery of all was that made by Adolf Deissmann, who
when studying transcripts of the Berlin collection of
papyri suddenly realised that the Greek which he was
reading was identical with the non-literary *koine* or
common Greek of the New Testament. Previously this
language had been regarded either as an indifferent
attempt to imitate the formal style of the earlier Classical
authors; as a distinct and separate form of Greek, as
Hebraic Greek, or even, as one scholar described it, "a
language of the Holy Ghost".[83] Now, thanks to the
labours of Deissmann, it is abundantly clear that the New
Testament was written in the vigorous language of
everyday life, and as such spoke simply and directly to the
hearts and minds of people from their immediate environment.

What is of equally great significance for the student of
the New Testament is the fact that there is no perceptible
difference between the style of the private letters written
in the first century A.D. and their counterparts from the
fourth century A.D. The longer letters generally opened

with a salutation, followed by thanksgiving and prayer for those to whom the letter was addressed. After this came the particular subject of communication, and then the letter closed with greetings or perhaps some prayerful utterance. As Milligan has shown,[84] these are the precise features which are found at a rather greater length in the letters of Paul, indicating that the Apostle was careful to observe many of the polite social conventions of his day.

A large proportion of the letters extant indicated the presence and activity of a scribe, who took down the letter by dictation. On some occasions when an amanuensis was employed, the one who was dictating would add his signature and a personal postscript, much as St. Paul did in the letter to the Galatian church.[85] A scribe who gave evidence of a fairly fluent style might well have been entrusted with the task of interpreting the mind of his employer in certain portions of letters, a practice which could account for recognisable differences of style and composition in the same document.[86]

The non-literary papyri of the early Christian era are clearly an indispensable source for the study of Christian origins. With their discovery it could well be said that, like the Master, the language of the New Testament has indeed risen from the dead.

Chapter II

SOME PALESTINIAN SITES

DESPITE the impact of western cultural patterns and modern technological developments upon the historic land of Palestine, there are still a great many features which have changed only slightly since the days of Jesus Christ. Among these are numerous sites and ways familiar to the reader of the New Testament, a large number of which are still readily identifiable by topographical, archaeological and other means. Maps of Palestine in the Roman period[1] indicated the extent of the military occupation, and also showed that the familiar system of Roman roads had hardly begun in the time of Christ. It was only after A.D. 70, when it became desirable for the tenth Roman legion to be in steady communication with Caesarea, the Imperial administrative centre, that the land was surveyed with a view to road construction. Prior to that time the roads were rough and haphazard in nature, being passable only in the dry seasons in a great many locations. Even the Roman road which enlarged the familiar route from Jerusalem to Jericho was not constructed until about A.D. 68.[2]

Of the sites which can be positively identified, Bethlehem is of interest as being the city of David and the birthplace of Christ.[3] Standing on a ridge in the hill-country of Judaea, it was about six miles south of Jerusalem in the fertile uplands which justified its ancient name "House of Bread". Under Herod the Great (37–4 B.C.), who instituted a vast building programme in Judaea characterised by architectural designs in the

Hellenistic tradition,[4] a large stronghold or Herodium was erected three miles south of Bethlehem. Access to this fort was gained by means of a long stairway, and the defensive towers which dominated it contained lavishly furnished apartments in which the king lived periodically.[5] When he died he was buried at the site,[6] the remains of which provide elequent testimony to the constructional activity of Herod the Great.

Another location which was the object of his attention was Samaria, the once proud capital of Omri and Ahab, which had been stripped of its stout defensive walls during the Maccabean period. In 30 B.C. Caesar Augustus formally presented the city of Samaria to Herod, who had married Mariamne there seven years earlier. By rebuilding and enlarging the city Herod endeavoured to consolidate his hold upon that part of the country, as well as doing honour to Caesar by renaming the city Sebaste[7] and dedicating a magnificent new temple to him.[8] Excavations at the site have shown that it was approached by a massive stairway leading to a platform flanked by pillars, behind which stood the temple proper. Near the foot of the stairway was an altar, and from the adjacent ruins was recovered a statue of Augustus.[9] The general plan of the shrine was typical of contemporary pagan temples, and it was probably the most imposing building in the entire city. To the east of the temple was a large open square surrounded by shops in the manner of most Hellenistic cities, while to the north of the mound but still within the fortifications was a rectangular stadium, enclosed in the Doric fashion with a roof supported by means of columns.

Of equal interest to Herod was Caesarea, which previously had been an unimportant site on the coast between Mount Carmel and Joppa. The king spent twelve years (25–13 B.C.) in making it into one of the most beautiful sites in Palestine. Although Caesarea has still to be excavated thoroughly, it is possible to see the Roman remains, which include a stadium, an amphitheatre, a marketplace, a temple and the remnants of the huge sea mole, some two hundred feet wide and one hundred and twenty feet deep, which was intended to make the harbour of Caesarea the equal of the port of Athens.[10]

A major effort of constructional activity, however, was expended upon the city of Jerusalem, which had sustained some damage during the Maccabean conflict and the regime of Pompey. The topography of the city had altered considerably since the time of David, so that the centre of Jerusalem in the first century B.C. was to the west and north of the Temple area, and not on the mound Ophel to the south. Thus it was impracticable to attempt to renovate the old Canaanite fortifications,[11] since there was a more pressing need for defences to the east and north-west. Two walls protecting these areas were already in existence when Herod became king, and he reinforced them with solid masonry and three huge defensive towers.[12] Just to the south of these fortifications he erected a magnificent palace[13] surrounded by canals and groves of trees.

At the north-west corner of the Temple area Herod rebuilt a Maccabean fortress and named it Antonia in honour of Mark Antony. According to Josephus[14] it was situated on the edge of a precipice about seventy-five feet in height, and boasted four strong towers on the corners. The fortress was well equipped, and a Roman cohort was always stationed there to prevent trouble in the crowded precincts of the Temple at the great festivals. It was to this structure that St. Paul was taken after being rescued from the fury of the Jewish mob by the timely intervention of the Roman soldiers.[15] L.-H. Vincent has suggested that the Tower of Antonia was the place where Jesus was tried by Pontius Pilate, basing his

views in part on the discovery of the pavement which
once covered the courtyard of the Antonia.[16] The paving
blocks were found to be of hard limestone, about a foot
thick and a yard square. If Pilate was actually in
residence in the Antonia fortress at the time when Christ
was arrested, it would constitute the Praetorium to
which Jesus was brought, and the courtyard pavement
would be the *Lithostroton* or the *Gabbatha* to which reference was made in the Fourth Gospel.[17] Of some interest
are the patterns scratched in the pavement stones in one
or two places, representing the play-board for a popular
game indulged in by the Roman soldiers.[18]

The major constructional achievement of the time of
Herod was unquestionably the extension of the second
Temple.[19] General repairs were carried out to the fabric
of the post-exilic structure, and the courtyard was greatly
enlarged so as to accommodate the vast crowds which
flocked to the principal religious festivals in Jerusalem.
In order to accomplish this aim it was found necessary
to build a platform, supported by vaults[20] and columns,
over an area to the south-east where the hill fell away
sharply. The platform was held in position by an enor-
mous retaining wall, parts of which are still clearly visible
at the present time. The lower courses are Herodian,
and consist of massive stone blocks, carefully hewn and
fitted together with a high degree of precision. On the
west of the Temple hill was the celebrated "Wailing
Wall",[21] where fourteen courses of Herodian masonry
can still be seen above ground level.[22] When completed
the Temple enclosure towered about two hundred feet
above the Kidron gorge at its outermost extremity,[23]
which added still further to the impressive nature of the
structure.

Herod enlarged the post-exilic Temple by adding
porticoes and cloistered courts flanked by splendid
colonnades. Beyond the gates of the Temple area

stretched a large courtyard known as the "Court of the Gentiles", and to the east of this lay "Solomon's Porch"[24] which was in need of considerable repair in the days of Herod Agrippa II.[25] Only Jews were permitted to pass from the Court of the Gentiles, where in all probability the money changers had their tables,[26] into the inner court. Josephus[27] described the stone partition which carried an inscription forbidding Gentiles to enter the inner court on pain of death.

Beyond the inner court were situated the Women's and Men's Courts, in addition to the Court of the Priests, near to which the sacrificial altar was located. In the innermost court stood the Temple proper, a magnificent structure of white stone decorated with gold.[28] It was unquestionably one of the most impressive edifices in the entire domain of Imperial Rome, and the renowned historian Tacitus was sufficiently gratified by the building to describe it as a "temple of immense wealth".[29] Well might the Rabbis exclaim, "He who has not seen the edifice of the Second Temple has not seen a handsome building in his life."[30] Unfortunately very little of this splendour can be studied at first hand today, owing to the thoroughness with which the Roman armies devastated Jerusalem in A.D. 70, along with the fact that subsequent buildings were erected on the site. In addition, Moslem veneration of the whole area precludes much in the way of archaeological activity, although a limited amount of such work can be undertaken periodically.

It is a regrettable fact that not all the traditional identifications of sacred places in Palestine are reliable. Thus Cana of Galilee[31] has been associated for many years with Kefr Kenna, four miles north-east of Nazareth. In actual fact Cana is the town of Khirbet Qana, some eight miles due north of Nazareth. The same is true of Capernaum,[32] where Jesus spent some time during His

Galilean ministry. This city was identified with a ruin
known as Khan Minyeh on the north-west shore of the
sea of Galilee. It is now apparent that a site further north
called Tell Ḥum is a more suitable location for ancient
Capernaum, since it is here that the remains of a fine
synagogue were uncovered,[33] which can be assigned
with confidence to a date *c.* A.D. 200.

On a slope in the Galilean hills lay the village of
Nazareth, where Jesus grew to manhood. At the foot of
the hill is the only source of water in the immediate
vicinity, to which Mary must have come with her water-
pot, as do the villagers of Nazareth to the present day.
This site is certainly one of the most assured locations
in Palestine, and in many respects life has changed there
but little since the days of Christ. Sepphoris, a neighbouring city, was a prosperous commercial centre in the
time of Herod the Great, and its strategic value was
considered to be such that during the uprising of A.D. 66
it was garrisoned by Roman soldiers. In 1931 the remains of a fort and a theatre, probably dating from the
period of Herod Antipas, were unearthed by archaeologists.[34]

The city of Jericho known to Christ was but a pale
shadow of the once-great Hyksos fortress, which prior to
the time of Joshua had occupied a strategic site of eight
acres in area, dominating access from the east into
ancient Canaan. Judging from the present nature of the
archaeological evidence there appears to have been an
occupational gap of about four hundred and fifty years
between the time when Joshua imposed a curse on the
site[35] and the defiance of that ban by Hiel the Bethelite,
about 880 B.C.[36] There are clear indications that considerable erosion of the site took place even before the
period of the Iron Age in Palestine, and this may have
contributed to a general lack of occupational interest
in Jericho prior to the seventh century B.C., despite its

favourable winter climate.[37] When Judah experienced the Second Captivity in 587 B.C., the inhabitants of the Jericho region were transported to Babylonia, and the mound[38] was never again settled to any significant extent.

In New Testament times the Jericho of Herod the Great had spread nearly two miles to the south-west of the Old Testament site in the direction of the Wadi Qelt. This move appears to have been the result of a distinct desire on the part of the inhabitants of Jericho to furnish an additional water supply to that found at the Ain el-Sultan.[39] Near the Wadi king Herod erected a magnificent palace patterned after the great Roman villas, and according to Josephus he also constructed a citadel called Cyprus,[40] a theatre,[41] and an amphitheatre.[42] The road from Jericho to Jerusalem[43] was about seventeen miles in length, and approached the Holy City through the Judaean hills and across the Mount of Olives.

The age in which Christ grew to manhood was one of political and religious ferment, as is clear even from a casual perusal of the history of those stirring times. It is against such a background that some attention must be given to the bearing of archaeology upon the Gospel narratives.

Chapter III

ARCHAEOLOGY AND THE GOSPELS

WHEN Alexander the Great died in 323 B.C., his empire was divided among his four generals. Seleucus I Nicator (312–281 B.C.) established the Seleucid kingdom in Syria about 311 B.C., and *c.* 200 B.C. his successor incorporated Judaea into the orbit of Seleucid rule. The Hellenizing policy of Antiochus IV Epiphanes (175–164 B.C.) provoked the Maccabean conflict, bringing temporary independence for Judaea. This terminated abruptly in 63 B.C. when Pompey made Syria a Roman province and brought Palestine as a whole within Imperial jurisdiction. In the west Julius Caesar (*c.* 102–44 B.C.) ultimately gained the political ascendancy after defeating Pompey at Pharsalus in 48 B.C., but he was unable to stem the tide of intrigue which swept the Empire and culminated in the rise to power of Octavian in 31 B.C. Four years later the title of Augustus was conferred upon the latter, and under his rule there began a prolonged period of peace for the turbulent Mediterranean area. In 40 B.C. Herod the Great came to terms with Augustus and was named king of Judaea. Towards the end of his life he ordered a census to be taken, and it was at this time that Jesus was born.[1]

St. Luke has supplied important historical material relating to this event in the statement that the Roman census resulted from a decree of Caesar Augustus, and that it was the first such enrolment under Quirinius, the governor of Syria.[2] St. Matthew, on the other hand, associated the incident in typically Jewish fashion with domestic events, placing the birth of Christ "in the days of Herod the king",[3] this Herod being identified as the father of Archelaus (4 B.C.–A.D. 6). In consequence a date of *c.* 4 B.C. would seem to be indicated by this evidence for the birth of Christ.

It should be noted that the Lukan reference to the census required that the population of the Imperial world of *orbis terrarum* was to be enrolled, but not necessarily in terms of a single census held on one specific occasion. In fact, as W. M. Ramsay pointed out long ago, the word used by Luke shows that Augustus laid down the procedure for systematic enrolment of the Roman world, and not for the taking of a single massive census.[4] That the machinery for such an administrative procedure was in fact operative seems clearly indicated in the writings of Clement of Alexandria (A.D. 155–220), who recorded that it commenced with the census which was in progress at the time when Christ was born.[5] Documentary evidence from Egypt, consisting of actual census papers for enrolments in A.D. 90, 104, 118, 132 and succeeding years is now to hand, and it is an accredited fact that in the later Empire there was a fourteen-year interval between enrolments.[6]

A census proclamation from Egypt, dated A.D. 104, indicates the general method adopted by the Roman authorities:

"Gaius Vibius, chief prefect of Egypt. Because of the approaching household census it is necessary to notify all those who are residing for any reason away from their own districts to prepare to return at once to their own governments, in order that they may complete the customary processes of the enrolment, and that the tilled lands may retain those belonging to them."[7]

The Romans clearly found it most convenient to assemble the various elements of the population in their places of

origin, and to enrol them by households. No doubt both
Mary[8] and Joseph were required by law to present themselves at Bethlehem, along with all others who claimed
that village as their birthplace. Equally certain is the fact
that they would have to file specific statutory declara-
tions and documents with the census officials. One such
form, deposited in the middle of the second century A.D.,
read as follows:

"To Julius Saturninus, officer of the Heracleopolite
nome, from Petesouchos son of Pisiotis, of the village
of Ancyronon. I make my return in the ninth year of
Antonius Caesar, the lord, in accordance with the order
of Valerius Proclus the prefect. Myself, Petesouchos
aged forty-two, my wife Tausiris daughter of Pareitis
aged thirty-four. Pnephorus my son aged seventeen.
I swear by the fortune of the Emperor that I have presented the aforesaid return honestly and truthfully,
and have told no lie nor omitted anyone who ought to
have been returned by me . . ."[9]

From about A.D. 150 comes an official notification of
birth, filed by a husband who was considerably older
than his wife:

"To Socrates and Didymus . . . scribes of the metropolis, from Ischyras son of Protas, son of Mysthes . . .
and from his wife Thaisarion, daughter of Ammonius,
son of Mysthes . . . of the same district. We register the
son who was born to us, Ischyras, being one year of
age in the present year, the fourteenth of Antonius
Caesar the Lord. I therefore present this notification
of birth. Ischyras, aged forty-four, without distinguishing marks. Thaisarion, aged twenty-four, without
distinguishing marks. Written for them by Ammonius,
scribe of the nome."[10]

Earlier scholars[11] objected that a census held by Quirinius could not have occurred in the time of Herod, since Quirinius had not then become governor of Syria.[12] However, it is clear from contemporary inscriptions that Quirinius exercised some kind of executive power on two distinct occasions in Syria. One of these sources, found at Antioch in Pisidia, spoke of "P. Sulpicius Quirinius duumvir" waging a campaign in Syria about 10 B.C.[13] in his capacity of "chief magistrate", while a second inscription[14] attested to his prominence in the Imperial army *c.* 6 B.C. It should be noted that Luke does not say that Quirinius held the census himself, but only that it was conducted at the time that he was legate. This is important in view of the observation of Tertullian[15] that Christ was born during the time when Sentius Saturninus was civil governor of Syria and Cilicia (8–6 B.C.). On the basis of the evidence to hand, the Classical scholar W. M. Calder concluded that Quirinius had held two governorships in Syria.[16] F. F. Bruce followed Ramsay in maintaining a date for the first of these between 10 and 7 B.C., and commented:

". . . there is substantial evidence that Quirinius held such a post at an earlier time, probably between 10 B.C. and 7 B.C. when as extraordinary imperial legate in the province of Syro-Cilicia for military purposes, he commanded an expedition against the Homanadenses, a mountain tribe of Asia Minor."[17]

The census may well have begun about 8 B.C., during the legateship of Quirinius and completed within the next two years, which would bring it within the lifetime of Herod the Great (*ob.* 4 B.C.), and at the same time harmonise with the statement of Tertullian.[18] This involves a slight readjustment of the traditional date of the birth of Christ, as has already been noted, a dating scheme which was first established in the early sixth century A.D.[19] While there are still certain unsolved problems connected with the general chronology of this period, the situation recorded in Luke 2:3 is, as Finegan has pointed out,[20] certainly quite plausible.

It has been suggested that the "inn" to which Mary and Joseph were refused admittance was the *geruth* mentioned in Jeremiah[21] as being near to Bethlehem and owned by one Chimham.[22] It is possible that this man, a descendant of the son of Barzillai,[23] had erected a hostelry in the time of Jeremiah for the benefit of travellers to and from Egypt, and that in New Testament times it was fulfilling much the same purpose. Being of Davidic descent, Mary might have expected to stay in the "guest-chamber",[24] but as it was already occupied she was offered the next best accommodation, a cavern cut into the rock with a raised platform at one end where visitors could sleep within sight of their belongings and their animals. The tradition that Christ was born in such a "stable" was firmly established by the time of Justin Martyr (*c.* A.D. 150), and about two hundred years later Constantine the Great built a church over this cave.[25] The present Church of the Nativity at the site has been rebuilt in large measure, but despite this, parts of the nave go back to the period of Constantine.[26]

Archaeology can throw very little light upon the life and ministry of Christ, if for no other reason than that the passing of the centuries has obliterated the bulk of the potential source material. From a reconstruction of the Second Temple and from information furnished by Josephus it is legitimate to assume that the presentation of the baby Jesus[27] took place at or near the door leading from the Women's Court into the Men's Court. The narrative of the Massacre of the Innocents[28] is in full accord with the later years of Herod the Great,[29] and the silence of Josephus on the matter can be explained by the fact that in all probability fewer than twenty children were involved in this sad episode. In the light of what is known about other grosser atrocities committed by Herod, this particular incident was from his point of view of a rather trivial nature.

Since public instruction in the Law and in Jewish religious traditions generally was given by custom in the Outer Court, it would probably be in this general area where Christ sat as a boy of twelve and entered into theological discussion with the doctors of the Law.[30] Luke alone of the Evangelists preserved the approximate age of Jesus when He commenced His public ministry,[31] and no record of the intervening years has survived. From the welter of hypotheses and conjectures concerning this period it seems permissible to assume only that Jesus worked for some years as a carpenter, and that when His putative father Joseph died He assumed the responsibility for providing a livelihood for Mary and His younger brothers and sisters.[32]

A reference in Luke[33] has furnished yet another attempt on the part of the author to date an event by reference to contemporary personages. On this occasion no less than seven synchronisms were given in order to establish the date when the ministry of John the Baptist commenced. Of the individuals mentioned, some question has been raised about Lysanias, named as tetrarch of Abilene near Damascus in the fifteenth year of Tiberius (A.D. 27–28).[34] For some time scholars identified him with an older Lysanias who governed neighbouring Chalcis from 40–36 B.C., but an inscription from the time of Tiberius named one Lysanias as tetrarch of Abilene,[35] while another recorded the dedication of a temple "for the salvation of the Lords Imperial and their whole household, by Nymphaeus a freedman of Lysanias the tetrarch".[36] Scholars now conclude that a younger and less famous Lysanias ruled over Abilene for a period of time, and that he was the person who was mentioned by St. Luke.

After having spent some time ministering in the Galilee region, Jesus returned to Jerusalem for a Jewish feast, probably a Passover celebration, and on this occasion He healed a chronically ill man at the Pool of Bethesda.[37] Not all the Greek manuscripts are in agreement concerning the rendering of the name Bethesda, and one ancient form, Bethzetha, has been associated with the area of Bethzatha to the north of the second wall of Jerusalem. A good deal of archaeological activity has been undertaken in the grounds of St. Anne's monastery in the vicinity of old Bezetha, and two pools lying many feet below ground level have been excavated. Traces of pillars in the immediate area have been assumed to be the remains of the Johannine "porches".[38] The Qumran Copper Scroll may contain a reference to the twin pools of Bethesda,[39] though in the opinion of the present writer this identification is by no means as assured as some scholars maintain.

Of the many contacts which Christ had with the Temple, the one on the last day of the Feast of Tabernacles[40] brought Him again into association with a pool, being on this occasion the celebrated Pool of Siloam, which conveyed water from the spring of Gihon into the Old City. The tunnel excavated by orders of king Hezekiah[41] was discovered in 1880, along with the famous inscription which described the operation.[42] The congenitally blind man whom Christ healed[43] was sent to the Pool of Siloam for symbolic washing.

Shortly before He died, Jesus had occasion to point to the ultimate futility of the constructional work being undertaken on the Second Temple,[44] and after that He went to Gethsemane for prayer. The modern visitor will be shown several sites which purport to be original, but in actual fact the location is not known. All that can be said with certainty is that the place where Christ prayed shortly before His arrest and trial was located on the western slope of the Mount of Olives, across the Kidron valley from Jerusalem. According to Josephus[45] the armies of Titus desolated Jerusalem for many miles around, making assured identification of the site an extremely unlikely prospect.

It is almost equally impossible to be certain as to the exact locations of the house of Caiaphas where Christ was taken,[46] the site of the Crucifixion,[47] and the place where Christ was buried in a garden-tomb.[48] However, there are some grounds for believing that the judgment before Pilate at the place of the "Pavement"[49] can be illustrated from archaeological discoveries, as was mentioned earlier. This "elevated place" has been associated by Vincent and others with a site in the Castle of Antonia just to the north-west of the present Temple area.[50] Patterns scratched on the surface of the large stones used for the pavement seem to be relics of a gambling game indulged in by the soldiers on duty. But if Pilate was residing at the palace of Herod rather than in the Castle of Antonia, the entrance to the palace itself, rather than the courtyard of Antonia, could have provided the Praetorium[51] on that occasion.[52] According to Josephus[53] the procurator Florus sat in judgment before the palace of Herod at a later date. While it is true that no pavement such as the one described in Mark has been uncovered in the general area of the palace, this is no indication that such a structure did not exist, or that it may not even yet come to light. If such a suggested location is proved to be correct, it will be clear that the procession from the residence of Pilate to Calvary did not follow the path of the traditional *Via Dolorosa*. At present, however, it is not possible to come to a definite conclusion on this point.

The first tangible evidence of the name of Pontius

Pilate, the Roman governor of Judaea, was uncovered in 1961 by an Italian archaeological expedition working at Caesarea, some ten miles south of Haifa on the east Mediterranean coast. Prior to that time the only testimony to the existence of Pilate consisted of the Gospel records and the writings of Josephus, but these sources have now been supplemented by archaeological evidence in the form of a stone slab some thirty inches by twenty-four inches inscribed with three Latin names, two of which are those of Pontius Pilate and the Emperor Tiberius.

Medieval identifications of sacred sites in Palestine are frequently far from accurate, and as has been observed already, present problems when attempts are made to locate such sites as Calvary and the tomb in the garden. If tradition is correct in locating the Church of the Holy Sepulchre on the hill of Calvary,[54] the second wall of the city, outside which the crucifixion took place, must have been situated to the east of the present church.

Traces of Herodian masonry can be seen on a course leading west from Antonia, and then going south to a point half-way between the Temple and the palace of Herod.[55] While this would permit the church to be outside the wall, a fortification built on this kind of pattern would be unsuitable for the defence of the city. An alternative suggestion would take the wall south and west of the Church of the Holy Sepulchre to a point just north of the palace, but this, too, has grave weaknesses from the standpoint of a defensive structure.[56] A third proposal has envisaged the wall extending to the north of Antonia and then following the course of the masonry levels subsequently erected by Hadrian, but this would bring the church inside the city wall. A final alternative follows a line west from Antonia in a semicircular direction to meet the first wall at the palace of Herod, but once again the Church of the Holy Sepulchre is included in this area.[57] The problem of identification is made more complex by the fact that traces of Herodian or earlier masonry can be found along all of the directional lines suggested, and as a result scholarly opinion is quite divided. It seems best to conclude that in the light of the present evidence it is not possible to identify the site of Calvary with any degree of certainty.[58]

Such tombs as have been assigned to the Herodian period appear to have varied from the small single grave carved out of the rocky hillsides to the much larger structures which provided for the interment of a number of corpses. The simplest arrangement consisted of an antechamber excavated from the rock wall, which led to a square chamber beyond in which the corpse was placed. In the case of a multiple tomb, three sides of the inner chamber contained horizontal shafts located above ground level (*kokim*), or else were fitted with narrow ledges recessed laterally into the rock (*arcosolia*). Access was gained through a low doorway which was closed by means of a stone door consisting of one or two leaves,[59] or alternatively by a large stone in a groove,[60] which because of its weight required considerable physical effort when it was being moved.[61]

The grave of Christ was of the *arcosolium* ledge variety, since it would be impossible for anyone to sit upright in the *kokim* type.[62] It was on such a ledge that the grave-clothes were doubtless deposited,[63] and this would make them readily visible from the vestibule without requiring actual entrance of the burial chamber itself.[64] Of considerable interest historically is the fact that the great stone slabs used for covering the entrances to tombs were in vogue chiefly from *c.* 100 B.C. to *c.* A.D. 100.

During the Roman period decrees were promulgated which prohibited the removal of the stone coverings of tombs and the mutilation of their contents. A slab of marble taken from a site in Nazareth in 1878 contained a

Greek inscription, possibly from the time of Claudius (A.D. 41–54), which stated:

> "Ordinance of Caesar. It is my pleasure that graves and tombs remain undisturbed in perpetuity for those who have made them for the cult of their ancestors or children or members of their house. If, however, any man lay information that another has either demolished them, or has in any other way extracted the buried, or has maliciously transferred them to other places in order to wrong them, or has displaced the sealing or other stones, against such a one I order that a trial be instituted, as in respect of the gods, so in regard to the cult of mortals. For it shall be much more obligatory to honour the buried. Let it be absolutely forbidden for anyone to disturb them. In case of contravention I desire that the offender be sentenced to capital punishment on charge of violation of sepulture."[65]

If the Nazareth edict did in fact emerge from the time of Claudius,[66] it may well have arisen as one result of the events which took place on the first Easter morning.[67]

Chapter IV

WITH PAUL THE TRAVELLER

AT the close of the last century it was a commonplace pronouncement of critical thought to ascribe the statements in Acts to "intentional deviations from historic truth in the interest of the special tendency which they possess".[1] This position was accepted at first by Ramsay, as was also the contention that the Book of Acts belonged properly to the middle of the second century A.D. However, as the result of a lifetime of archaeological research in Asia Minor and elsewhere, he came to the conclusion that Acts "must have been written in the first century and with admirable knowledge"[2] by one who was "among the historians of the first rank".[3]

Despite the evidence which Ramsay adduced for the authenticity and historical accuracy of the Book of Acts, a number of European scholars have remained unconvinced. As Morgenthaler has pointed out,[4] the trustworthiness of Luke as an historian has been opposed on the ground that his work has to do with artistic rather than historical considerations, and also that his testimony is of a theological rather than a primarily historical order. He himself concluded that Luke was narrating a redemptive history which involved the historical (*geschichtlich*) event of redemption but which was not history as commonly conceived. Haenchen took a similar view in his commentary on Acts,[5] maintaining that Luke was especially interested in safeguarding the theological continuity between Israel and the Christian Church. In order to maintain such a position, he alleged, it was necessary for Luke to depart to a significant extent from events as they really happened.

A more conservative approach was adopted by Gärtner,[6] who pointed out that St. Luke viewed the trend of events from a religious standpoint, which was evident from his record of the speeches in Acts. However, he maintained that while Jewish rather than Greek historiography was the motivating methodology, some reliance could be placed on the historical settings for the speeches in Acts. Ehrhardt also held that Luke followed the Jewish tradition of historical biography, but maintained a high view of Luke as an historian, asserting that he employed written sources in recording what really happened.[7]

While it is true that Luke as an historian reflects to some extent the traditional Semitic approach to historical data, there can be no question that of all the Evangelists he most nearly approaches the standards of the Classical historians.[8] Thus the elaborate synchronism which marks the beginning of the Third Gospel proper[9] is in complete accord with the literary pattern followed by Thucydides in the *Peloponnesian War*.[10] The historiography of St. Luke is typical of the Hellenistic age, and ranks with the work of Polybius, Josephus, Plutarch and Tacitus. Some of the most impressive examples of Lukan accuracy consist of the titles of Imperial officials recorded in his writings.[11] That these reflect the contemporary scene is evident from the fact that the titles of provincial governors changed without warning when the status of particular provinces was altered. Failure to appreciate this important circumstance has proved embarrassing for unwary commentators, and has led to a variety of needless critical conjectures. Precisely how accurate Luke was as a recorder of the contemporary scene will become apparent shortly.

The importance which the Third Evangelist attached

to the conversion of Saul of Tarsus for the growth and
development of the Christian Church can be gauged
from the fact that he included three accounts of it in the
Book of Acts.[12] His meticulous descriptions of places and
events in the life of that colourful and vigorous Apostle
of the Christian faith must accordingly receive some
attention. Luke made it clear that Antioch in Syria,
where the disciples were first called Christians,[13] played
a significant part in early Christian history. According to
Josephus,[14] Antioch was the third city of the Empire
after Rome and Alexandria, and the modern town of
Antakiyeh is but a shadowy counterpart of its illustrious
precursor. Excavations at the site[15] uncovered the island
on which one of the more important districts of the city
had been built, and revealed the presence of two cemeteries of the second century A.D. Also excavated was the
circus, a structure which was reputedly one of the largest
and most celebrated of its kind in the entire Roman
empire.

From Antioch the Christian community sent help to
the poor in Jerusalem, who had been experiencing great
hardship because of a food shortage which occurred in
the days of Claudius Caesar (A.D. 41–45). According to
Suetonius[16] his reign was marked by *assiduae sterilitates*,
which resulted in famine prices for produce. Dio Cassius
and Tacitus also mentioned two famines in Rome,[17]
while Josephus[18] related that Queen Helena of Adibene
brought food from Egypt and Cyprus to relieve famine
conditions in Judaea during the procuratorships of
Cuspius Fadus and Tiberius Alexander (A.D. 44–48).
Thus the visit made by Paul to Jerusalem was most probably the one mentioned in Galatians.[19] Despite the importance of Antioch for early Christian history, the
remains of churches so far discovered at the site only date
from the fourth century A.D. A mosaic floor from the
sixth century A.D. bore the following inscription:

"Peace be to your coming in, you who gaze (on this);
joy and blessing be to those who stay here."[20]

Though Antioch once boasted a large Jewish colony
which included numerous Greek converts, the mosaic
inscription and a marble fragment with a portion of a
seven-branched candlestick on it are the only remains
discovered to date of the Jewish inhabitants of Antioch.
By far the most celebrated artefact from the area is the
"Chalice of Antioch",[21] whose discovery was announced
in 1916 by G. A. Eisen.[22] A plain inner silver cup measuring nearly eight inches in height and about six inches in
width was surrounded by an outer gilded shell exhibit-
ing the figures of Christ and the Apostles.   Eisen dated
the decorated holder within the last third of the first
century A.D., but other scholars have assigned it to a
date between the second and sixth century A.D.[23] Although some questions have been raised as to the authentic nature of the artefact,[24] it seems probable that it is an
early piece of Christian art, though not from the first
century A.D.

About A.D. 46 the Church in Antioch sent Paul and
Barnabas on the first missionary journey, and in company
with John Mark they sailed to Cyprus,[25] some sixty miles
distant. The island first appeared in historical records
when it was captured by Thutmose III of Egypt,[26] and
at a later time it was inhabited successively by the
Phoenicians and the Greeks. The Romans occupied it
about 58 B.C., and after 22 B.C. its governor was given
the title of proconsul. An inscription from the year
A.D. 55, uncovered just north of Paphos, contained
the phrase "in the time of the proconsul Paullus".[27]
This is the only surviving extra-Biblical reference to
this proconsul, and it is of some interest that St. Luke
furnished his name and designation with complete precision.[28]

From Cyprus Paul and his companions entered the southern part of the extensive Roman province of Galatia, which was subdivided at that time into several regions including Pisidia, Phrygia and Lycaonia.[29] The name Galatia originated with a group of European Gauls who occupied the northern area in the third century B.C. When their last king died about 25 B.C., Galatia was incorporated into the Empire, and the Roman free city of Antioch which had been founded originally by Seleucus I of Syria about 300 B.C. became the chief civil and military centre of the province. Here Paul and Barnabas preached the Gospel with considerable success, despite the prevalence of a wide variety of pagan religious groups in the region. Just prior to the First World War Ramsay excavated the ruined site of Pisidian Antioch and uncovered the great temple dedicated to the deity Men. Near the ruined altar were the remains of a great many bones of sacrificial animals. An inscription which mentioned "Lucius Sergius Paullus the younger" was taken by Ramsay as a reference to the son of the proconsul of Cyprus.[30] Subsequent work at the site[31] brought to light further remains from the time of Augustus, including some excellent examples of first century A.D. sculpture and architecture which reflected a combination of Roman solidity and Greek refinement.

When trouble arose in Antioch, the Apostles moved to Iconium, Lystra and Derbe, which lay to the south-east of Antioch but were still in the same political region. Iconium, a Hellenistic city of some antiquity, was situated on the border between Phrygia and Lycaonia, and ancient writers commonly assigned it to one or other administrative district.[32] Luke, however, makes it abundantly clear that Iconium was in Phrygia as far as political considerations were concerned, and that in passing to Lystra Paul crossed over the frontier.[33] Equally correct is his description of Lystra and Derbe as two large

towns of Lycaonian Galatia.[34] The site of Lystra was
discovered in 1885, and was found to contain an ancient
altar still standing in its original position and bearing a
legible Latin inscription which gave the name of the city
as Lustra.[35] The discovery in 1926 of a stone altar dedicated to Hermes and the "Hearer of Prayer"[36] has
illuminated the action of the enthusiastic inhabitants of
Lycaonia in comparing Paul and Barnabas with Mercury
and Jupiter.[37] Apparently the worship of these two
deities had been incorporated into the local cultic rites,
as was indicated by an inscription from nearby Sedasa
which recorded that a statue of Hermes was dedicated to
Zeus by a group of people who bore Lycaonian names.[38]
The author of the Acts of the Apostles was clearly well
informed about all these matters.

With the return of Paul and Barnabas to Antioch in
Syria the first missionary journey ended, and some time
after the Council of Jerusalem[39] Paul wrote his letter
"unto the churches of Galatia". To address the churches
of Pisidian Antioch, Iconium, Lystra and Derbe in this
manner would be perfectly correct, for it would refer to
communities within the Roman province of Galatia.[40]
Some scholars, however, have preferred to locate the
churches in north Galatia proper,[41] which while strictly
correct ethnographically does not accord with the situation described in Acts, and in consequence must be
rejected.

The second missionary journey[42] commenced with Paul
and Silas passing through Syria and Cilicia to the province of Galatia, where they were joined by Timothy.[43]
The close economic relationship of Lystra and Iconium[44]
was noted incidentally by St. Luke,[45] who furnished
further topographical information when he spoke of Paul
crossing over into a new district described as "the
Phrygian and Galatian region".[46] This designation was
most probably used in the popular sense of the border

area between Phrygia and Galatia, that is to say, "the district which is both Phrygian and Galatian".[47]

Archaeological excavations at Philippi have done much to clarify the account of the visit made by Paul to that city.[48] Founded in the middle of the fourth century B.C. by Philip of Macedon, it passed under Roman control along with the rest of Macedonia in 168 B.C. Brutus and Cassius were defeated by Antony and Octavian in a battle fought in the vicinity in 42 B.C., and when Octavian conquered Antony and Cleopatra at Actium in 31 B.C., the city received the title of *Colonia Iulia Augusta Philippensis*. Excavations at the site were conducted by the École Française d'Athènes prior to the Second World War,[49] and uncovered the remains of the forum, the acropolis, the Roman baths and the theatre.

The designation of Philippi in Acts as the "first of the district" had occasioned considerable comment on the part of scholars, particularly since the Greek word *meris* was not employed to describe a "region" or "district". But when the Egyptian papyri were discovered it became clear that *meris* was a common first century A.D. designation for "district",[50] particularly in Macedonia. While the local capital was Amphipolis,[51] Philippi had already begun to surpass it in importance. Ramsay made the situation clear when he wrote that "Amphipolis was ranked first by general consent, Philippi first by its own consent."[52]

The "gate" at Philippi mentioned in the Lukan account[53] is most probably to be identified with the ruins of a great arched gateway unearthed to the north-west of the city proper. This structure appears to date from the first century B.C., and may have symbolised the status of the city as a Roman *colonia*. The Via Egnatia passed westward through this archway, and about a mile beyond Philippi it crossed the river Gangites (Ganga). If the gateway actually served to mark the point beyond which alien deities were forbidden to pass into the city, it would account for the fact that the Jews were compelled to meet on the other side of the gate near to the river Gangites.[54]

Luke quite accurately designated the local officials of Philippi as "praetors".[55] While it was customary for the magistrates of Roman colonies to be known as "duumvirs" rather than "praetors", it is clear from Cicero[56] that in educated circles the latter was a courtesy title for the magisterial officials of the colony. Yet another example of precision in the use of titles concerned the "politarchs"[57] of Thessalonica, the city to which Paul journeyed after leaving Philippi. Inscriptions from that region have now shown that the term "politarch" was used of magistrates in Macedonian cities some nineteen times from the second century B.C. to the third century A.D. One inscription over the Varder Gate which stood originally at the western entrance to the city of Thessalonica, commenced, "In the time of the Politarchs . . ." This inscription has been assigned to a period between 30 B.C. and A.D. 142, and is one of several which mentioned the politarchs.[58]

From Macedonia Paul travelled alone to the province of Achaia, and waited in Athens until his companions arrived.[59] Excavations in this celebrated city have done much to recapture the splendour of its massive architecture and magnificent Classical sculpture. Of particular interest to the readers of the New Testament is the unearthing and restoration of the ancient *agora* or marketplace, which was the centre of Athenian civic and commercial life.[60] It was situated some distance to the northwest of the Acropolis, and was enlarged in the time of Julius Caesar and Augustus. In this *agora* Paul spent some time discussing the implications of the Christian faith with the Jews and others prior to the arrival of Silas and Timothy.[61]

The Areopagus, from which Paul delivered his address to the assembled philosophers,[62] was a rocky hill nearly four hundred feet in height, and situated somewhat north-west of the Acropolis.[63] In antiquity it was the meeting-place of the Areopagus Council, which had complete authority in political and religious matters alike. Under the Romans the court was charged with educational responsibilities, and the Council took its name from the place where it assembled.[64]

The reference in the Areopagus address to an altar bearing the inscription "to an unknown God"[65] is in complete accord with the observations of Paul concerning the superstitious religiosity of the Athenians.[66] While no inscriptions containing the precise wording mentioned by the Apostle have yet been found at Athens, such inscribed altars were by no means unknown in various parts of Greece at that period, as indicated by contemporary writers.[67] An altar recovered from the temple of Demeter at Pergamum in 1909[68] bore a legend somewhat as follows:

> "To unknown gods,
> Capito,
> Torch-bearer."[69]

The last important town which Paul visited on his second missionary journey was Corinth, the flourishing commercial and political centre in the Roman province of Achaia, where the Apostle stayed for some eighteen months and founded a church. The excavation of Corinth was made possible by a devastating earthquake in 1858, which caused the old city to be abandoned in favour of a site nearly four miles to the north-east. The American School of Classical Studies at Athens has worked for many years at the site,[70] and has shown that the earliest occupational levels go back to the fourth

millennium B.C. In 146 B.C. it was badly damaged by
the Imperial armies, but in the following century a
Roman colony was established in the area, and reconstruction was still in progress during the days of St. Paul.
As Broneer has pointed out,[71] Corinth was the most
advantageously located city in the whole of Greece for
the evangelistic purposes envisaged by St. Paul, with its
flourishing mercantile trade, its multitude of visitors to
the Isthmian games, and its pagan indigenous population
which included a thriving Jewish colony.

Excavations near the Lechaion Road, which led into
the *agora* from the north,[72] uncovered the remains of
several workshops opening out on to the street or courtyard, similar in style and construction to the one in
which Paul worked at his trade with Priscilla and
Aquila.[73] At the foot of the broad stairway or Propylaea
which led to the *agora*, a long block of stone inscribed in
Greek lettering was unearthed in 1898. The script was
badly mutilated,[74] but it was restored to read, "Synagogue of the Hebrews",[75] and was dated by Adolf
Deissmann[76] between 100 B.C. and A.D. 200. It now
seems probable that the inscription is later than the time
of St. Paul,[77] although the synagogue in which he
preached was probably in the vicinity.

Each of the shops which opened out on to the *agora*
had its own well, connected by an underground channel
to a supply of fresh water, which would help to cool
and preserve perishable commodities. In one of these
shops the excavators discovered a doorstep which bore
the inscription, "Lucius the butcher."[78] The Latin word
macellum was the same as that used by Paul to describe
the meat-market or "shambles" of Corinth.[79] It should
be noted, however, that other areas of this ancient city
may well have possessed similar establishments where
meat was sold.

The *agora* at Corinth was built on two levels, and in the

centre of a terrace which separated the lower area to the north from the higher portion to the south was an elevated platform or "judgment seat".[80] It was to this place that Paul was taken by the Jews of Corinth to be judged by Gallio, the "deputy" of Achaia. An inscription found at Delphi spoke of Gallio as proconsul of Achaia,[81] indicating that he took up his position in either A.D. 51 or 52. Since Acts implies that he had only recently become proconsul, it would point to a date of about A.D. 50 for the arrival of Paul in Corinth. Luke thus once again furnished a correct title for the local Imperial official.[82] The action of Gallio in supporting freedom of speech seems, as Ramsay remarked,

" . . . to pave the way for Paul's appeal a few years later from the petty outlying court of the procurator of Judaea, who was always so much under the influence of the ruling party in Jerusalem, to the supreme tribunal of the Empire."[83]

North-west of Corinth, in the vicinity of two ruined theatres, a paving-block bearing an inscription in Greek was uncovered by American archaeologists. It stated that the pavement was the work of Erastus, who was at that time the *aedilis* or Commissioner of Public Works.[84] This official is generally identified with the Erastus who became associated with Paul in the spread of the Gospel,[85] and who was referred to in Romans[86] as the *oikonomos* or "chamberlain" of the city.

The phraseology of the letters to the Corinthian church frequently reflects the intimate knowledge of the people and their way of life which the author possessed. These little glimpses included references to the work of the shepherds and agricultural labourers,[87] feasts in pagan temples,[88] and the celebration of the Isthmian games.[89] As Broneer has commented:

"In the pursuit of his calling Paul had made it his practice to visit every quarter of the city and to be present at every kind of occasion when men gathered for work or play, and he spoke to them not as an outsider but as one of their own people. A perusal of the ruins of ancient Corinth and of the abundant archaeological material gathered in the museum cannot fail to add force and vividness to the homely figures of speech with which the Apostle Paul sought to impress his message upon his hearers."[90]

After a protracted stay in Corinth,[91] Paul left for Ephesus with Priscilla and Aquila on his way to Jerusalem. He was to visit the city again for another extended ministry on his third missionary journey, about A.D. 53.

Chapter V

THE GROWING CHURCH

HAVING reported to the church in Jerusalem,[1] Paul set out hurriedly for Galactic Lycaonia and Phrygia. When he had visited the churches in this region he came to Ephesus where he spent more than two years of his third missionary journey[2] in evangelistic work and in establishing the church at Ephesus on a firm spiritual basis. The city itself was the principal one in the Roman province of Asia, and had been settled as early as the seventh century B.C. by Asiatic tribes. In the fourth century B.C. it came under the control of Alexander the Great, and when Antiochus III was defeated by the Romans about 190 B.C., it was governed by Eumenes II, who erected the splendid Altar of Zeus[3] at Pergamum. In the time of St. Paul, Ephesus had become the chief commercial centre of Asia Minor,[4] and ranked in greatness with Alexandria and Antioch in Syria.

Ephesus was well known for the cult-worship of the mother goddess Artemis, whom the Romans associated with Diana, and it was the desire to locate and identify the temple of this goddess which prompted the first exploration of the site in 1863 by the English architect J. T. Wood. After six years of work traces of the temple wall were discovered to the north-east of the city proper. A Roman inscription from the time of Trajan (A.D. 98– 117) described several gold and silver images of Artemis[5] which were to be placed in the temple and carried in procession on the birthday celebrations of the goddess.[6] Subsequent excavations[7] have revealed the entire history of the Artemisian shrine, which from rather unelaborate beginnings blossomed into the magnificent Hellenistic temple of Alexander the Great, an edifice which measured over one hundred and ten yards in length and about fifty yards in width. The temple boasted one hundred columns approximately fifty-five feet in height,[8] while the main altar was about twenty feet square. The entire building was decorated with marble tiles, sculpture, paintings and gold leaf, making it a colourful and splendid religious centre even by Greek standards.[9]

Perhaps the riots mentioned in Acts[10] coincided with the month of Artemision, when crowds of tourists and worshippers thronged Ephesus in order to participate in the religious ceremonies held during that season. The theatre to which Paul was taken was another of the imposing structures of ancient Ephesus, and from the remains which were uncovered it seems most probable that the theatre could accommodate at least twenty-four thousand persons. It was linked with the harbour of Ephesus by means of a paved marble street known as the Arkadiane,[11] which was lined on each side with a colonnade to give added dimension and elegance. The "town clerk", a native of Ephesus who was responsible to the Roman provincial administration for the general behaviour of the citizenry, quelled the riot by reminding the milling crowd of the heavenly origin of Artemis,[12] and the fact that she had honoured Ephesus by bestowing the title of "Warden of the Temple of Artemis"[13] on the city.

The reference to magicians[14] reflects the popularity of the occult arts at Ephesus. The formula, "I adjure thee . . ." was a regular part of exorcist rituals, and certain extant magical papyri have been found to contain the Divine Name variously pronounced as *Iao*, *Iaoue* and *Iae*.[15] The term "deeds"[16] was employed in a technical sense to denote "magical formulas". Inscriptions from Ephesus frequently contain the title "Asiarch",[17] which served to designate a leader in the provincial cult of Emperor-worship. Normally the office was held for one year only, but the title was usually retained after the holder retired from his position, thus making for several Asiarchs at any given time.

Shortly after the disturbance at Ephesus, perhaps in the summer of A.D. 55, Paul left for Macedonia. When he had spent a short time in Greece, during which he again saw the elders of the church at Ephesus,[18] he returned to Caesarea, and from there journeyed to Jerusalem. It had been the firm intention of the Apostle for some time to pay a visit to Rome, as indicated in the letter to that church in the Imperial city,[19] a document which was most probably written from Corinth during his visit there on the third missionary journey. As events transpired, Paul went to Rome as a captive, having appealed from the authorities in Judaea to the justice of the Imperial court by virtue of his Roman citizenship.

The immediate accusation levelled against Paul by his Jewish adversaries was that he had brought non-Jews into the "holy place",[20] in direct contravention of strict Jewish religious custom. The Herodian Temple contained several notices placed at intervals in the precincts of the building, warning Gentiles against trespassing on or entering areas which were reserved specifically for Jews.[21] One such inscription was discovered by Clermont-Ganneau in 1871, and is now in the Istanbul museum. It contained several lines of Greek letters, and may be translated as follows:

"No Gentile may enter inside the enclosing screen around the Temple. Whoever is caught is alone responsible for the death which follows."[22]

A long-standing difficulty concerning the account of the harbour of Phoenix (Phineka) in Crete now appears to have been solved. Luke described the harbour as facing north-west and south-west,[23] whereas modern Loutro in the Cape Mouros area, the only safe harbour in southern Crete, actually faces east.[24] This led Ramsay[25] to suppose that Luke had somehow misunderstood the Pauline account of the majority decision aboard ship. The situation appears to have been clarified by the work of R. M. Ogilvie,[26] who discovered traces of two inlets in the long-disused bay. One of these is now covered over as a result of earthquake disturbances in the region, and faces north-west, while the other is heavily silted and faces south-west. From the available evidence it would appear that the western bay constituted the harbour in Classical times.

The designation of the Roman governor of Malta as "first man"[27] has been shown to be correct by the discovery of two Maltese inscriptions. One was written in Greek[28] and the other in Latin,[29] and taken together they constitute still further evidence of the accuracy with which St. Luke designated local Imperial officials.

Paul landed in Italy at Puteoli,[30] which was not far from Pompeii,[31] and followed the Via Appia in the direction of Rome, some one hundred and fifty miles distant. The *forum Appii* or Market of Appius where Paul was greeted by "the brethren"[32] was about forty miles from the Imperial capital, while the *Tres Tabernae* or Three Taverns was a village about ten miles further along the Via Appia. Precisely where St. Paul was imprisoned when he arrived in Rome is difficult to say. According to an ancient tradition he was incarcerated in the old State prison known as the Carcer Mamertinus, situated on the northern edge of the Capitoline Hill, though naturally this cannot be substantiated for sheer lack of evidence.

The earliest traces of active Christianity in Rome are to be found in the numerous cemeteries along the roads leading from the city,[33] and also in underground chambers or catacombs. Jewish catacombs, some of which date from the first century A.D., were frequently marked by means of religious symbols, and those which have been recovered included the *menorah* or seven-branched candlestick. Christian catacombs were also found to be decorated with symbols, one of the most common being the fish, whose letters stood in abbreviated form for "Jesus Christ, Son of God, Saviour."

Traditionally both Peter and Paul were martyred in Rome under Nero between about A.D. 64 and A.D. 68. The burial place of Paul was located by second century A.D. tradition on the Ostian Way,[34] while Peter was supposed to have been laid to rest under what is now the altar of St. Peter's Basilica in Rome.[35] In 1941 a series of excavations took place under the altar when a tomb was being provided for Pope Pius XI, and beneath the levels of the Constantinian church, erected in the early fourth century A.D., were discovered two rows of mausoleums containing Roman burials. Beneath the memorial built by Constantine over the traditional grave of Peter was an earlier structure, which appears to have been erected about A.D. 160.

At an even lower level were some burials which may have dated from A.D. 70. One of these contained the bones of a man of apparently powerful physique, and this led some to speculate on the possibility that perhaps at long last the remains of St. Peter had been uncovered. In the nature of the case it is, of course, quite impossible to make such an identification, despite the presence elsewhere in the immediate vicinity of a charcoal drawing of an old man with the letters PETRUS beside it.[36] The most that can be said at this stage is that the memorial under the altar of St. Peter's Basilica is probably a cenotaph which may mark the general location of the grave of Peter without, however, specifying the exact place of interment.

While the extant writings of Paul and Peter reflect accurately the contemporary linguistic forms of *koine* Greek, their treatment of certain words exhibits a distinct departure from secular usage, particularly as represented by the Classical period. It is by no means difficult to understand this development in the circumstances, since words need something more than ordinary significance if they are to express the riches of the indwelling Christ. Thus it is not surprising that the Apostles frequently employed the *koine* vocabulary, familiar from the papyri, in a new and distinctive manner when describing the spiritual life of the Christian in its manifold aspects. By raising that which was common to greater heights of grandeur and power, they were conveying a graphic illustration of the true nature of that transforming faith which they were attempting to propagate by every means possible.

This tendency can be illustrated by reference to the word "Gospel" itself. During the Classical period it was frequently used of the reward given to one who brought good tidings,[37] and also of the thank-offering made when good news had been received.[38] For the Christian it signified the good news of Divine redemption and salvation in Christ.[39]

The verb "to baptize" is another instance of the conversion of that which was secular and profane to strictly religious usages. In Polybius[40] it was used of soldiers wading breast-deep in water, and of ships sinking at sea. In a more ordinary sense it signified one who was drenched,[41] or metaphorically, of one who was soaked in wine[42] or head over heels in debt.[43] It was also employed of the act of drawing wine by dipping the cup into the wine-bowl.[44] In the vocabulary of the Christian it described the sacramental act of initiation into the fellowship of the Church.[45]

An even more dramatic example of the converting

power of the Christian faith as applied to the phraseology of that day is seen in connection with the word which is usually translated "humility."[46] While the term did not occur very often in common speech, it was invariably used to describe a base or mean-spirited person,[47] a sense which even occurred in the writings of Josephus.[48] In one of the papyri[49] the word was used of a mean act. At the very most the concept of "humility" signified for the Classical writers a sense of modesty which was thought seemly for females only, and was certainly not a quality to be found in the character of a virile male. Christianity transformed this word, and elevated it to the status of a sovereign grace to denote the proper attitude of the Christian towards his Saviour and society at large.[50]

The way in which certain words were used in the Greek papyri has served to illumine their meaning in the New Testament writings. Thus the term "earnest"[51] was commonly employed in *koine* Greek to describe a down-payment, as a preliminary to the balance being discharged in full at a subsequent time. One papyrus stipulated that certain dancing-girls engaged for a village festival were to receive some money as an advance payment of their salary,[52] where the word "earnest" was used in precisely the New Testament sense of an advance bestowal of what will be fully completed later on.[53]

In those papyri which recorded commercial dealings, the word for "seal" commonly occurred, either to describe a silver seal, a signet ring, or a seal impression.[54] As a verb it was employed in the technical sense of sealing up bags of wheat and barley in order to make proper delivery.[55] It was against such a background and with such a precise usage in view that St. Paul, in writing to the church in Rome,[56] informed the believers that all the appropriate steps regarding the collection for the poor in Jerusalem had been taken, and that he, like an

honest merchant, would see to it that the delivery was
properly effected. Of the many examples which it is
possible to cite, the foregoing will serve to indicate the
way in which the popular idiom was consistently
adapted and transformed by New Testament writers in
order to describe some new spiritual experience or
dimension.

Archaeological investigations have shed some light
upon the conditions mentioned in the Book of Revelation. Sir William Ramsay studied the location of the
seven churches described in the earlier chapters of that
book, and concluded that they represented seven postal
centres on a circular route, each of which was meant to
receive and read the particular letter addressed to it.[57]

For its witness in the midst of a pagan society the
church in Ephesus received some commendation,[58]
although it was urged to repent and intensify its evangelistic activity. Smyrna, which was situated on a deep
gulf some thirty-five miles north of Ephesus, was an
early rival of that city in matters of culture, trade and
commerce. It was founded about 1100 B.C. as a Greek
colony, by the Aeolians, but was soon taken over by the
Ioanian Greeks and incorporated into the Ioanian
League. Early in the sixth century B.C. king Alyattes of
Lydia conquered the region and destroyed the old city.
For over two centuries the site was sparsely populated,
but at the beginning of the third century B.C. Smyrna
was refounded and fortified by Antigonus and Lysi-
machus in its present location. The patron deity of the
city was the mythological Amazon Smyrna, who was
regularly depicted in the short tunic and high boots of
the hunter-warrior and carrying the double-headed
axe of the Amazons.[59] About 195 B.C. Smyrna declared
decisively for the Romans, and never wavered subsequently in her loyalty to Imperial rule. For this the city
was rewarded in 23 B.C. by the Roman Senate, which

chose Smyrna over ten other cities in the province of Asia for the privilege of erecting a temple to the emperor Tiberius.

References in Classical literature to the "crown of Smyrna" seem to point to the floral garland worn in the cultic rites of the goddess Cybele, which were long cherished as a source of local pride. The reward of a "crown of life,"[60] promised in the Book of Revelation, would therefore be particularly apt for Smyrna, since the church would thus wear an adornment suited to the faithful servant of the living God.

Pergamum, fifty miles north of Smyrna, was the focal point for several religious cults, notably that of the Greek healing deity Asklepios. Coins unearthed at the site frequently bear the symbol of a serpent, which was sacred to the Asklepiad cult. Pergamum was the first provincial town to have a temple dedicated to the deified emperor Augustus (A.D. 29), and by the time of Severus (A.D. 193–211) two other similar shrines had been erected there. Excavations in and around Pergamum since 1878[61] have revealed something of the majesty and splendour of this ancient seat of Imperial government.

On the summit of the rocky crag which dominated Pergamum, an altar to the Greek deity Zeus had been erected in antiquity. This structure was recovered by German archaeologists and taken to Berlin, where in recent years[62] it was set up in the Eastern sector of the city. Perhaps the reference to "Satan's Seat"[63] was to the cult of Imperial worship in general, and to the altar of Zeus in particular.

Thyatira, a small inland town situated between Sardis and Pergamum, was also a cultic centre whose guardian deity was Apollo, the sun god. Founded about 300 B.C. by Seleucus I, the town grew into an important commercial capital whose trade guilds were more numerous

than those of any other city in Asia.[64] Many inscriptions
recovered from the site mention the variety of trades in
Thyatira, speaking particularly of works in wool, linen,
garments, leather, pottery and bronze.[65] The Christian
church in that city was rebuked for its lack of resistance
to the pagan cults, and the representation of the Son of
God[66] stands in marked opposition to the image of
Apollo, son of Zeus, and the statues of the Emperors.

Sardis, which lay thirty-five miles to the south of
Thyatira, had formerly been the capital of Lydia. King
Cyrus conquered it in 546 B.C. when Croesus, king of
Lydia, was defeated, and in later times it fell under
Seleucid control. The patron deity of the city was
Cybele, in whose honour several shrines were built.
Excavations which commenced in 1910 uncovered the
ruins of the principal Cybele-Artemis temple,[67] which
proved to be the outstanding architectural relic of the
site. To the north of the city the archaeologists discovered eight large piers of white marble, which have
been thought by some scholars to constitute the remains
of a church. More assured in this connection is the small
brick structure adjoining the south-east angle of the peri-
style of the pagan temple, which has been assigned by
archaeologists to the fourth century A.D. This is much
the best preserved of the Christian remains at Sardis, and
though there may well be other ruins of earlier churches,
more intensive excavational activity would be necessary
before any specific religious structure could be identified
as such and related directly to the period envisaged in the
Book of Revelation. The Christian church in this ancient
centre was urged to repent and be faithful to its Christian
commission.[68]

Philadelphia, nearly thirty miles south-east of Sardis,
was the focal point of a thriving wine industry. Its
strategic geographical location made it a doorway into
central Phrygia, and so the church in that city was

commanded to be an "open door" in Christian evan-
gelisation.[69] Apart from a few inscriptions and some
coins, little of value either for the archaeologist or the
student of the New Testament has been recovered from
the site.

Laodicea, approximately forty-three miles to the
south, was another bustling commercial centre in antiquity, but according to the Book of Revelation[70] it was
in an impoverished spiritual condition. Very little
excavation has been undertaken at the site, which unfortunately has been progressively denuded by the local
inhabitants. Dr. M. J. S. Rudwick and E. M. B. Green
have thrown some light on the description of the Laodi-
ceans as being lukewarm rather than either cold or hot.[71]
In visiting the site in 1956 they showed that of the towns
in the locality, only Laodicea possessed no natural water
supply, having to rely entirely upon the hot springs near
Denizli. They discovered traces of the end of an ancient
stone aqueduct which had been constructed in order to
bring water from Denizli into Laodicea. The hot water
would become progressively cooler as it neared its
destination, being lukewarm when it finally reached the
city.[72] Because it shared this characteristic, the church
in Laodicea was charged with ineffectiveness rather than
sheer indolence or lack of zeal.

The enigmatic enumeration of the Beast in the Book of
Revelation[73] to designate an individual has been
paralleled by a number of similar inscriptions from the
same general period. These arose in the first place from
the fact that the letters of the Greek and Latin alphabets,
like those of the Hebrew in the Maccabean period, were
assigned numerical values, and as a result they were
commonly employed in the making of puzzles and
cryptograms. From Pompeii came an amusing inscription scratched on a wall, which when deciphered read,
"I love a girl whose number is 545."[74]

In the Book of Revelation the problem is made more acute by the presence of one manuscript variant which reads 616 instead of 666.[75] In Greek, 616 adds up to "Caesar God", but 666 fails to yield any such name. On the basis of similar numerical values in the Hebrew alphabet, it is possible, with only a slight irregularity, to arrive at the name "Nero Caesar" as the equivalent of 666.

It may well be that the number of the Beast is deliberately represented as falling short of 777, the complete Trinity, embodying the ancient Semitic idea of seven as the symbol of perfection, thus presenting a graphic picture of the imperfection and wickedness of the Antichrist.[76] Archaeological illustration of the concept which may underly the image of the seated woman[77] has been furnished by a coin of the emperor Vespasian, which represented Rome as a woman seated upon the seven hills of the city.[78] It is not too much to hope that additional discoveries will assist in understanding the significance of the imagery in this rather obscure document of early Christian history.

Chapter VI

QUMRAN AND THE NEW TESTAMENT

WHEN the discovery of the Dead Sea scrolls[1] was announced to the scholarly world in 1948,[2] it was widely believed that, because of their nature and contents, the documents could be expected to throw most light upon the history of the Old Testament text. In the event this expectation was amply justified, but as many more manuscripts and fragments were found at Qumran and neighbouring sites, and as the character of the religious brotherhood emerged both from an examination of such documents as the *Community Rule* (1QS) and the excavation of the *khirbeh* itself, it became increasingly apparent that the emphasis was shifting into the area of New Testament studies. This movement was precipitated by statements from one or two scholars to the effect that the Qumran discoveries necessitated a radical revision of traditional thought with regard to the origins of Christianity. The resultant debate formed what van der Ploeg, who was associated with the early discoveries at Qumran, has called, "the most inglorious chapter of the communication of the finds in the desert of Judah to the general public."[3]

The French scholar A. Dupont-Sommer was the first to make a statement which purported to see a startling resemblance between the Righteous Teacher, the ostensible founder and leader of the Qumran brotherhood, and Jesus of Nazareth,[4] a viewpoint which he modified somewhat as the result of subsequent discussion.[5] In 1956 John Allegro, who was preparing some of the Qumran Biblical texts for publication, announced in the course of a lecture transmitted by the British Broadcasting Corporation[6] that previously un-published texts from Qumran showed that the Righteous Teacher had been crucified by Alexander Jannaues (103–76 B.C.), and that his disciples expected his resurrection. Thus the leader of the Qumran sectaries anticipated the fate which ultimately overtook Jesus of Nazareth somewhat more than a century later.[7]

The furore which this statement aroused was modified considerably by the publication of a letter in the London *Times*,[8] written by five other members of an inter-national team of scholars engaged in the study and publication of the scrolls, in which they declared that, on further reading of the documents in question, they found nothing to support the contentions of Allegro, and concluded that he had either misread the texts or fabri-cated a series of conjectures which were totally un-warranted by the nature of the evidence.

Public interest was aroused in the United States by an article on the Qumran scrolls which appeared in *The New Yorker* in 1955. Written by Edmund Wilson, a distinguished journalist and literary critic, it was sub-sequently expanded and published in book form[9] after Mr. Wilson had visited the Qumran area and discussed the whole topic with several scholars.

Wilson expounded the extreme view of Dupont-Sommer, and gave it as his opinion that the rise of Christianity should be understood simply as an episode of human history rather than as dogma and divine revelation.[10] Thus the characteristic teachings of Christianity had emerged gradually from a dissident sect of Judaism, and were not as unique as so many of their adherents had been claiming down the centuries. Wilson managed to convey the impression that scholars were so stunned by the implications of the Qumran scrolls for faith and doctrine that they were suppressing information about the contents of the manuscripts discovered to date.

That the latter allegation is completely without foundation is evident from the rapidity with which the major Qumran documents were made available in photographic form to the world of scholarship.[11] More serious, however, was the charge, repeated in a book by A. Powell Davies,[12] that theologians lacked the courage to confront the historical and doctrinal implications of the scrolls, and were greatly disturbed as to the outcome of study on the problem as a whole.[13] The fact of the matter is simply that some of the most talented Biblical scholars of our age have examined the Qumran material scientifically and dispassionately, taking pains to consider a far wider range of evidence than was available when Dupont-Sommer made his initial pronouncements on the relationship of the Qumran community to Christianity.

One result of this scholarly activity has been the unanimous agreement that Dupont-Sommer and Allegro derived their views partly from untenable translations and forced interpretations of their source material. Another is that the observations of Wilson were not merely premature, but were based upon a methodology which would never be entertained for one moment in Wilson's own field of literary criticism. It is now clear that his approach transposed matters of relative historical fact into the realm of absolute theological values by enquiring as to the extent to which the doctrines of the Christian faith would need to be changed or abandoned, instead of ascertaining factually the relationship between the teachings of Christianity and the tenets of the Qumran sect. Even more serious was his assumption that the interim pronouncements of one scholar could be taken as representing the considered judgment of scholarship as a whole, a method of procedure which is as disastrous as it is unfortunate.

Finally, it is completely fatuous for Wilson to suppose that the only persons qualified to furnish an objective and informed opinion regarding the initial Qumran discoveries are scholars without formal religious affiliations. Biblical scholarship has long attained to that level of maturity which enables important issues relating to Judaism and Christianity to be discussed objectively without the participants feeling that faith was thereby being shaken to its very foundations. Against the challenge that New Testament scholars were suppressing information concerning the contents of the Dead Sea scrolls, or were consistently refusing to consider the issues raised by those documents, it need only be stated that such men are now in the forefront of research in the field of Qumran studies, as a collection of essays, published only two years after the book by Wilson, can testify amply.[14]

From those scrolls which describe the discipline and doctrines of the sect, it is immediately apparent that it had certain elements in common with early Christianity. The Qumran community was based upon a New Covenant, which not merely involved all that Moses and the Law had taught,[15] but also demanded of its adherents a genuine response in penitence and faith to the revealed will of God.[16] A strict way of life characterised the organisation of the community, the aim of which was to attain to the standards of holiness, equity, justice and mercy as revealed in the Divine nature.[17] Their leader was believed to have been especially endowed with prophetic insight,[18] and it was partly on this account that the sectaries devoted a good deal of time and attention to the prospect of a Messianic advent[19] based to some extent upon the promises given to Moses in Deuteronomy.[20] A collection of Messianic proof-texts recovered from the fourth Qumran cave[21] outlined the concepts of the community on this particular subject.[22]

A document known as the *Rule of the Congregation*[23] described a banquet scene at the dawn of the new Messianic age in which the participants were assembled in order, and the bread and wine were eaten after being blessed by a priest[24] and the Messiah.[25] The fact that the ritual could apparently be followed at any time seems to imply a definite sense of sacramental communion with the Messianic figures as well as a degree of anticipation of those events which would result in the establishing of the Divine kingdom.[26]

That great importance was attached by the sect to ceremonial washings[27] has been shown by the excavation of large cisterns at the site of the Qumran community settlement. One such pool had been cut deeply into the rock, and had fourteen stone steps at one end which gave full access to the water at the various levels.[28] While the ritual lustrations at Qumran seem to have had much in common with the baptismal practices of contemporary sects in Judaism, it is clear that the lay brotherhood placed particular emphasis upon the spiritual implications of such rites. The *Rule of the Community* taught that spiritual repentance alone determined whether or not the rite was ultimately efficacious,[29] and emphasised that only by complete submission of the will to God could the individual be cleansed, since the application of water could not by itself achieve that effect.[30]

At first sight it might appear that not only have the two distinctive Christian sacraments been anticipated by the communal life at Qumran, but that this applies also to certain aspects of organised life in the early Christian church such as the Twelve Apostles[31] and the presbyters of the first century A.D.[32] In this connection one has to be careful to avoid the logical fallacy known as *post hoc ergo propter hoc*, to which writers such as Wilson and Davies have fallen victim. This position assumes that if

Jesus and Christianity came later than the Righteous Teacher and the Qumran fellowship in point of time, and if similarities between the two can be demonstrated clearly, the origin of Christianity is thereby explained, and its alleged uniqueness can be dismissed accordingly.

What must be understood clearly is that both the Qumran sectaries and the early Christians inherited the vast wealth of Jewish religious tradition, so that if one is able to identify doctrinal or other antecedents under such conditions, it obviously can have little or no real bearing upon the validity of the Christian claim to uniqueness. In point of fact it is only when the differences between the thought and practice of the Qumran fellowship and the first century A.D. Christians are noted that one is able to appreciate clearly the distinctive nature of the Christian religion.

Like the Qumran sectaries, the early Christians espoused a New Covenant, but it was one achieved through the atoning blood of the Messiah,[33] who was acknowledged as having come in the person of Jesus Christ. While the sectaries esteemed the Servant oracles of Isaiah highly,[34] their Messianic thought did not include the work of a compassionate Servant who would be numbered with the transgressors and would bear the sins of many. Although the scene in which the Christian sacramental meal was initiated is similar in points of detail to the apocalyptic Messianic banquet described in the Qumran texts, it associated the New Covenant with the shed blood of Christ, symbolised by the cup of wine,[35] in a manner which was completely foreign to the theology of the Dead Sea sectaries. The memorial character of the Christian meal has no counterpart either in the Qumran literature or, for that matter, in Essene practice, since the meals of the latter were most probably not sacred in character at all, and included food other than the elements of bread and wine. In the same manner the concept of the mystical presence of the Saviour in the heart of the believer who commemorates the Atonement by means of a celebration of the Lord's Supper is a development which is completely missing among both the Qumran sectaries and the Essenes generally. The sacramental meal whose institution is described in the New Testament followed the celebration of the traditional Passover rites,[36] and pointed to Christ as the promised Lamb of God who should atone for human sin by dying on Calvary.

Whatever functions the Messiah might have been expected to exercise in the dawning of the kingdom, it is apparent that the Qumran brotherhood never expected him to die for human sins, for they regarded it as their peculiar task to adopt the role of the suffering servant of God so as to effect expiation for the sins of their fellow Jews. Indeed, the sectaries had no concept whatever of universal sin, for this was essentially an individual affair.[37] When the human mind had been illumined by means of the twin spirits of truth and light, a person began to follow the path which culminated in salvation. Against this theological background a Messianic atonement for the sin of mankind was clearly both undesirable and unnecessary.

While there is an obvious element of anticipation common to the liturgical enactment of the apocalyptic Messianic banquet at Qumran and the celebration of the Lord's Supper,[38] the theological presuppositions which underly them are seen to be vastly divergent in nature. A final difference is that the meals were not envisaged against the same concept of worship on an assigned day of the week. According to a rubric which prescribed the procedure to be followed for the Qumran Messianic banquet, it could apparently be celebrated whenever a quorum of ten men happened to be present, which, as Cross has remarked, was presumably the current

practice of the sect.[39] Although the Qumran brotherhood, as well as other groups of an Essene nature,[40]
may have held sacred feasts from time to time on the
analogy of Jewish sacrificial meals, there is no evidence
that these repasts corresponded to the Last Supper or the
Eucharist of early Christianity to any significant extent.

The ceremonial washings in which the Qumran
brotherhood engaged appear to have been similar in
character to those which obtained amongst other Jewish
religious groups just prior to the beginning of the Christian era.[41] Such lustrations were of periodic incidence,
and were profoundly symbolic in nature, pointing as they
did to repentance and amendment of life. The sectaries
taught that no *ex opere operato* efficacy attached to the
rite, since it was only a truly penitent mind which could
avail for the transgressor.[42] A related monastic order, the
Covenanters of Damascus, which has striking affinities
with the Qumran group and with which it is identified
by many scholars,[43] prescribed an adequate amount of
clean uncontaminated water for ritual purification,[44]
and preferred a rock cistern as a container to any smaller
vessel. While such stipulations were obviously of importance for the Qumran community, these "volunteers for
holiness" sought as their ultimate goal that bestowal of a
new outlook and the outpouring of the Divine spirit long
promised by Ezekiel,[45] of which ceremonial lustration
was but the outward and visible sign.

Because they believed that they alone exemplified the
true Israel whose sins had been blotted out through
obedience to the ordinances of God, the sectaries were
convinced that they excelled all others in their apprecia-
tion of the spiritual significance of the rite. They taught
that the Divine spirit cleansed from sin, and that the
penitent worshipper would undergo increasing experi-
ences of sanctifying grace to the point where a direct act
of Divine favour at the Judgment would complete the

entire process satisfactorily.[46] From the Qumran writings it also appears that the sectaries credited the Messiah with baptism by the Holy Spirit of God in order to forestall contamination by evil powers,[47] since it was the express task of the Messiah to "sprinkle many nations"[48] and extend the same privileges of sanctification to His anointed followers.[49]

The Qumran literature contains no specific prescriptions as to the manner in which the purificatory rites were to be carried out, and since ceremonial washings were a common occurrence amongst the sectaries it may well be that more than one particular pattern was followed. It seems most probable that all that was necessary was an adequate amount of water and a willingness on the part of the participant to conform to the general principles of the *Rule of the Community* in the absence of precise directions concerning methods and techniques. This situation may be a reflection of the freedom from prescribed ritual patterns which prevailed amongst other contemporary baptist sects in Palestine, with the result that an act of baptism could be regarded as completely valid sacramentally whether it was the result of immersion, affusion or some other method of application.

The earliest Christian baptismal rites probably differed but little from their counterparts in Judaism, where the baptism of proselytes was an important element in the reception of the individual into the fellowship of Judaism. The ritual activity in which John the Baptist engaged was described in the Gospels as a "baptism of repentance",[50] and it is possible that the individuals who submitted to it were partly immersed and then had water poured over their heads in order to complete the sacramental act. As a Christian rite baptism was given greater theological content by being related as a symbol of the operation of Divine grace to the personage of the Divine Trinity, and also by being restricted in incidence to a single occurrence in the life of the believer.

It is here, of course, that the most significant difference from the Qumran ritual practices emerges, for the sectaries knew nothing of Trinitarian theology. For them, as has been noted, baptismal ceremonies were of a periodic nature, and formed a necessary part of the sanctifying process in the individual experience. More particularly, because the sect was of a highly esoteric order, the lustrations were restricted to those members who were fulfilling the obligations to which they had pledged initial allegiance. Thus the thought of baptizing every nation in the triune Name, which is so prominent in the Christian commission, constituted an evangelistic concept which was not merely foreign, but completely abhorrent to the thought of the Qumran brotherhood.

Occasional references are made in the Gospels to the Judaean wilderness, a large, inhospitable tract of land in which the Qumran settlement was located. The public ministry of John the Baptist commenced in Judaea,[51] and it was here also, in some area whose identification is not as yet absolutely certain, that Jesus Christ spent the traditional forty days of His temptation.[52] On another occasion Jesus passed a few days of quiet fellowship with His disciples in the lovely Judaean countryside bordering the wilderness immediately prior to His last visit to Jerusalem.[53] These, along with other considerations, seemed to confirm in the mind of Edmund Wilson the thought that Khirbet Qumran, rather than Bethlehem or Nazareth, was in fact the cradle of Christianity.[54] In a similar vein a distinguished archaeologist wrote:

"John the Baptist was almost certainly an Essene, and must have studied and worked in this building (*at*

Qumran); he undoubtedly derived the idea of ritual immersion, or baptism, from them. Many authorities consider that Christ Himself also studied with them for some time. If that be so, then we have in this little building something unique indeed, for alone of all the ancient remains in Jordan this has remained unchanged—indeed, unseen and unknown, to this day. These, then, are the very walls He looked upon, the corridors and rooms through which He wandered and in which He sat."[55]

Because of the background from which they have emerged, suggestions and hypotheses of this kind deserve more than a passing glance. In the case of John the Baptist, the account in the Gospel of St. Luke[56] indicates that as a boy he left his home in the hill-country of Judaea and went into the desert to pursue an ascetic way of life "until the day of his showing unto Israel."[57] During this period nothing is known of his activities, and when he reappeared to commence his ministry he manifested the attributes of an ascetic prophet[58] who advocated and practised a baptism of repentance[59] which had in prospect the approaching Divine kingdom.[60]

It has been suggested by those who think that John the Baptist had some kind of contact with the lay brotherhood at Qumran or with a religious group of a similar character[61] that since his birthplace was quite near to the Qumran settlement, he had in fact been adopted and brought up by the sectaries under the provisions which permitted them to train children and incorporate them into full membership as adults.[62] If the community was actually Essene in character, which, however, is by no means certain despite the opinions of many scholars, this step would not constitute anything of a particularly unusual nature,[63] since the importance which the sect accorded to priestly families[64] might have encouraged Zacharias, the father of John the Baptist, to send his son to an Essene community for his religious training. It is true that the message of repentance which John proclaimed had much in common with the tenets of the brotherhood at Qumran, which regularly spoke of itself as "those who repent of transgressions"[65] and who were living in a "covenant of repentance".[66] Again, the emphasis which John laid upon the necessity for true repentance as a prerequisite to spiritual cleansing and renewal was much akin to that found in the Qumran literature.[67]

John regarded himself as a forerunner of the Messianic age, much as the sectaries did,[68] and as a "voice crying in the wilderness"[69] rather than as the Messiah Himself. Whereas John baptized with water, the Messiah would baptize with the Holy Spirit[70] and with fire.[71] John further interpreted his work of preparation against the background of a desert sojourn and an ascetic way of life which had many obvious points of contact with the ideals of the Qumran community.[72]

But despite the fact that it is very difficult to reconstruct with complete confidence the life and teachings of John the Baptist from the rather general references to him in the Gospels, it is apparent that certain significant differences in theory and practice existed between John and the Qumran sectaries. Whatever connection he may have had with the lay fellowship during his youth, he emerged from the desert as a stern individualist who was quite evidently not connected with any specific religious group.[73] He seems in general to have avoided social contacts, preferring to remain in the desert where he taught his disciples,[74] without, however, attempting to organise them into a sect after the Qumran or some other pattern. Thus there is very little evidence for the statement made by Cross that,

". . . it is quite likely that the members of his sect formed congregations, and, like the Essenes and early Christians, constituted themselves a community of the elect, baptized in repentance and in anticipation of the imminent New Age."[75]

In his attitude John the Baptist gave no hint of being satisfied with the Qumran communal ideal, for so far from pursuing esoteric rites in a sheltered religious environment, he chose to take his message to the house of Israel and come into contact with sinners, an attitude which was completely alien to the "Purity of the Many" at Qumran. His dissatisfaction with the way in which the sectaries were endeavouring to fulfil the promises of Isaiah[76] by preparing themselves only, and not the nation as a whole, for the Messianic coming would be reflected, if he was at all familiar with the tenets of the brotherhood on this point, in his teachings concerning baptism. Whereas at Qumran the lustral rites were of periodic incidence and an essential element in the process of sanctification, as has been noted earlier, John proclaimed a baptism which demanded that the house of Israel as a unit should be purified against the time when the promised Anointed One should come. It is impossible in the nature of the case to state whether or not there was any significant difference in technique between the baptism of John and the lustral rites at Qumran. However, it is most probable that the former was a single occurrence for those who participated in it, whereas it was a consistent element in the piety of the sectaries.

Despite the great emphasis placed upon baptismal rites in the Qumran literature, there is nothing which would suggest that the brotherhood required initiates to undergo a baptism of repentance for the forgiveness of sins, and this attitude constituted a position far removed from that of the Baptist. In the light of any supposed connection between John and the Qumran sectaries, it is rather ironical that the Baptist alone was privileged both to recognise the true Messiah of Israel[77] and to have his devotion used for the dawning of the New Age, in view of the fact that the covenanters of Qumran were dedicated to preparing the way which the Messiah was expected to follow. In conclusion, it can only be remarked that any association between John and the Qumran sect, as based on the known desert experience of the Baptist, is at best hypothetical. The most that can be said for certain at present is that there appear to be some points of contact between the preaching of John, on the one hand, and a few of the theological tenets of the Qumran community and Palestinian Essene groups generally on the other.

If it is difficult to associate John the Baptist with the activities at Qumran, it is even more precarious to attempt such a procedure in the case of Jesus. By His own admission Christ was not an ascetic,[78] and while He fasted periodically He did not compel His disciples to follow His example.[79] As far as is known, Christ passed His childhood continuously in the Galilee region, apart from an occasional festal visit to Jerusalem. Even His period of solitude in the wilderness during His temptation, the traditional site of which is some twelve miles north-west of Qumran, would have afforded little opportunity of initiation into the wisdom of the sectaries, assuming that such a procedure was either necessary or desirable. In actual fact there is absolutely no evidence to suggest that Christ was ever associated with the Qumran covenanters in any way, and even less proof that He was at one time a student receiving instruction in their hallowed halls. As F. F. Bruce has remarked,

"If, in the course of His wilderness temptation, He was tempted (as seems certain) to achieve His messianic destiny by other paths than that of the Suffering Servant, marked out for Him at His baptism, then among those other paths which He repudiated the way of Qumran, in many of its aspects, must be included."[80]

An analysis of the Qumran literature indicates a number of impressive parallels to the teachings of Jesus,[81] but despite this, a good deal of caution must be urged before conclusions are reached. New Testament scholars have for long been well aware of the fact that almost every element in the ethical teaching of Jesus can be paralleled in the Rabbinic literature.[82] Lest this should be taken as an occasion for alarm at the prospect of the uniqueness of Christ and the Divine authority of Christianity being imperilled once more, it need only be remarked that the Qumran sectaries, the Rabbinic authorities, and Jesus Christ alike drew upon a common tradition of Divine revelation as contained in the books of the Old Testament. Under such conditions it would be rather surprising if there were only a few points of contact, since the devotion of Judaism and the Qumran brotherhood to the Law was more than matched by the attitude of Christ, who came not to destroy the Law, but to fulfil it.[83]

On this basis it is permissible to indicate a measure of similarity between some of the eschatological phrases used by Christ and their counterparts in the literature of Qumran concerning the Last Days. In 1QS,[84] a passage which described the condition of the righteous at the day of judgment stated that all iniquities would be forgiven in order to enable the sinner to contemplate the light of life. There appears to be comething in common here with the words of Christ as reported in the Fourth Gospel,[85] where those who follow the Saviour shall not walk in darkness, but shall have the light of life. The negative attitude of the sectaries towards money can be illustrated by the aphorism, "They rolled in the paths of whoredom and in wicked gold,"[86] and by the assertion, "I desire not the gold of unrighteousness,"[87] both of which are distinctly reminiscent of the injunction of Christ to his followers that they could not serve God and mammon at the same time.[88] But from the narrative of the man who was healed of a withered hand on the sabbath day,[89] and the rebuke administered to the Pharisees about rescuing on the sabbath day a sheep which had fallen into a pit, it is clear that both Christ and the Pharisees were unwilling to comply with the instructions of CDC, which stated explicitly that "if it (*the animal*) falls into a pit, it may not be removed on the sabbath."[90]

In general it must be said that parallels from the Qumran literature to the phraseology of Christ are almost entirely restricted to the fifth chapter of St. Matthew's Gospel.[91] The much-discussed expression "poor in spirit"[92] can no longer be held to mean the '*am ha'areç* or "people of the land", the vast group of little and despised folk,[93] but in the light of the designation which the sectaries applied to themselves as "the poor",[94] it must be understood as the "faithful" in spirit, or better, "the spiritually loyal", since the community regarded itself as the sole true witness in the world to the Divine revelation.[95]

The *logion* forbidding a man to be angry with his brother without a cause[96] may be paralleled by the concern expressed in 1QS for brotherly love to constitute a dominant feature of the community life: "Let no man bring something against his brother before the many if he has not already admonished him before witnesses."[97] This procedure was similar to the method suggested by Christ for dealing with a delinquent brother.[98]

The provision in connection with adultery[99] was also paralleled by the Qumran concept of self-denial, as is illustrated by the following phrases: "stubbornness of sinful heart and eyes of unchastity",[100] "a spirit of wantonness",[101] "those who do not lust after their eyes",[102] and "whoredom by taking two wives during their lifetime."[103] The sectaries adopted the same position as that taken by Jesus in His controversy with the Pharisees on the indissolubility of marriage[104] when they said, "The basic principle of creation is 'Male and female created He them'."[105] The rejection of oaths by Jesus[106] was paralleled by Essene thought as reported by Josephus,[107] and also by the Qumran covenanters, who laid down the principle that "It is forbidden to swear by God's name El, and by God's name Adonai."[108] The rather unusual statement in Matthew[109] about not resisting evil but turning the other cheek has somewhat of a counterpart in the Qumran literature, where one of the sources stated: "I will not repay a man with evil, I will follow the man of power with good, for God has judgment over all life, and He repays each according to his works."[110]

In the realm of eschatology it is apparent that some of the tenets of the lay brotherhood at Qumran had much in common with the teachings contained in the Gospels and other portions of the New Testament on matters involving the final judgment and eternal salvation.[111] The covenanters laid great stress on the Messianic sections which occurred in the writings of the Old Testament prophets, and there is some ground for thinking that they occasionally associated the personage of the Suffering Servant of Isaiah[112] with that of the Messiah without, however, regarding the Servant as being identified with sinners and bearing the iniquities of the human race. One passage, which depicted the community itself as representative of the Servant ideal, spoke of the council of Twelve as expiating wrongdoing by the performance of just deeds and by living a life of asceticism.[113]

In the light of the Qumran Messianic expectation, any attempt to identify the Righteous Teacher with Christ must obviously be less than adequate. If the Righteous Teacher can be regarded as an individual and not just in terms of a continuing office, it is abundantly clear that there are vast differences between Christ and the ostensible founder of the Qumran community. The Righteous Teacher was never regarded in the Qumran writings as a Messianic personage in any sense, and was not expected to atone vicariously for the sins of the world by his death. Indeed, so far from being Divine, he himself was a sinful man who needed Divine grace in order to live a good life. His teachings were sectarian, and he did not manifest any one of the marvellous works so characteristic of the incarnate Christ. As van der Ploeg has put it:

"That Jesus of Nazareth was an astonishing reincarnation of the Teacher is completely out of the question. If, however, one were to suppose that this were after all true, there would still be no reason for any Christian's being disturbed. Because Christians believe that Jesus is risen from the dead and is the Son of God: and they recognise this as the predominant and decisive difference between Him and the still anonymous Teacher. The Teacher did not rise from the dead, nor is he Son of God like Jesus."[114]

If John the Baptist was associated in some manner with the Qumran sect, it could account in part for certain linguistic expressions and thought-forms of the Fourth Gospel. The earlier chapters of this work in particular contain many words and phrases common to the *Rule of the Community*,[115] and this has led some scholars to reappraise the old tradition that John the Evangelist had been a disciple of John the Baptist.[116] Thus the *logos* concept of St. John[117] can be paralleled to a certain extent by the following passage:

"By His knowledge everything has come into being, and everything that is He has established by His purpose, and apart from Him nothing is done."[118]

Although there is no attempt to equate purpose and knowledge theologically with the Word, the correspondence in other directions is quite close.

Additional elements of the Johannine vocabulary found in the diction of the sectarian literature include "children of light",[119] "life eternal",[120] the "spirit of truth" and the "spirit of error",[121] "walking in the light" and "walking in the darkness",[122] "the light of life",[123] "works of God",[124] and numerous other characteristic expressions. The occasional note of hostility towards "the world" in the Johannine writings[125] is paralleled by the Qumran injunction to "hate all the children of darkness",[126] The phrases "that they may be one", "that they may become perfectly one"[127] are Semitic forms whose structure is matched closely by the diction of Qumran,[128] which elsewhere stressed the unity of the sect.[129]

However, while the Evangelist drew upon terminology which was also current at Qumran, it is clear that he was at variance with a good many of the interpretations and doctrines characteristic of the sectaries. Thus, whereas John could speak of the "children of God" and the "children of the devil"[130] as well as the "spirit of truth" and the "spirit of error",[131] there were many other occasions on which he was obviously not in theological agreement with the Iranian dualism so typical of the *Rule of the Community*.[132] His divergence from the fundamental tenets of Qumran thought is evident from the fact that his propositions were firmly rooted in the Hebrew

religious tradition, which upheld metaphysically a
monistic concept of reality whose ultimate principle was
transcendently good rather than evil.[133] Furthermore,
John exhibits a characteristic difference from the theology of both Judaism and Essenism[134] in emphasising
Divine grace as revealed in the Cross, rather than supporting a mechanical adherence to the works of the Law
as the sole means of human salvation.

These conclusions will ultimately have an important
bearing upon critical theories regarding the origin of the
Johannine traditions. Already it is increasingly apparent
that there is less evidence than was formerly imagined
to support the claims of Gnostic influence upon John.
The same holds good also for the view that the Johannine
writings generally took their rise within the Philonic
dualism of Alexandria.[135] As Montgomery remarked
nearly half a century ago concerning the Fourth Gospel:

". . . the Gospel of John in the composition of a well-
informed Jew, not of the Pharisaic party, whose life
experience was gained in Palestine in the first half of
the first century, and whose mother-tongue was Aramaic; and that this conclusion alone explains the
excellence of the historical data and the philological
phenomena of the book."[136]

In the view of certain scholars, some portions of the
Qumran literature have been taken as illuminating the
organisational beginnings of the primitive *ecclesia*.[137]
Much debate has been expended upon the problems
associated with the nature of church government in
Apostolic times, and various writers have concluded that
the original and basic form was congregational,[138]
presbyterian[139] or episcopalian,[140] according to their
ecclesiological preferences. In point of fact it would
appear that elements of all three types are represented

in the New Testament, and that a freely democratic, congregational order gradually moved in the direction of a more fixed monarchic pattern. In the Apostolic age there seems to have been little if any distinction between bishops (*episkopoi*) and elders (*presbuteroi*), both being interchangeable as indicated by the Book of Acts,[141] where Paul assembled the elders of the church of Ephesus and addressed them as *episkopoi* (overseers or bishops),[142]

At Qumran the three priests were assisted by overseers or *mebaqqerim*[143] as well as the twelve laymen who formed part of the community council.[144] These "overseers" would appear to correspond to the "presbyters" of Apostolic times, and among the sectaries the office was, with that of the presiding priest, one of the highest to which the members of the religious community could hope to attain. The "overseer" presided over the sessions of "the Many", and exercised the offices of treasurer, director of sacred and secular labour, and supervisor of candidates for admission to the brotherhood. He was required to be devoted to the welfare of his charges "as a father loves his children", shepherding them in time of trouble.[145] The concept of the shepherd as descriptive of leaders and overseers was an established Old Testament theme,[146] and thus it is not surprising to read that Jesus spoke of Himself as "the good shepherd"[147] and that one of His disciples applied the concept of the Christian Shepherd to Him.[148]

While there would thus appear to be a distinct consonance between early Christian ecclesiastical organisation and the administrative patterns of the Qumran sectaries with their democratic assembly, the council of twelve and the episcopal overseers, it is clear from the New Testament that the primitive Church exhibited several significant differences. In the first instance whereas the sectaries were at best expositors of the Law and custodians of the rites, ceremonies and mysteries of the brotherhood, the disciples of Christ were living witnesses to a unique personage, Jesus, the incarnate Messiah of God, who by a vicarious atonement had redeemed mankind and had brought justification and salvation within the reach of every sinner. As St. Paul expressed it,[149] they were ministers of Christ and stewards of the Divine mysteries, who witnessed to a quality of spirituality which was at once intensely personal and sacramental, and for which parallels are completely lacking in the Qumran scrolls. Furthermore, the exclusive nature of the monastic community demanded that there should be a continuing divergence between Jew and Gentile, whereas in the early Church this difference was eliminated resolutely by consistent emphasis upon the unity found in Christ.[150] Finally it should also be noted that the functions of bishops in the early Church differed widely from those ascribed by the Qumran literature to the *mebaqqerim*.

Although it can be pointed out that there are obvious parallels between the communal way of life at Qumran and the sharing of worldly goods in the primitive Church, it should be recognised that the differences are equally notable. The concept of fellowship inherent in the term *yaḥad* as used in the scrolls is strongly reminiscent of the *koinonia* of the Apostolic age, but the theological connotation is somewhat different. The fellowship of Christians embraced Jews and non-Jews alike; it was closely associated sacramentally with the second coming of the ascended Christ, it had an immediate practical outreach in terms of the social work which was undertaken among the poor and the destitute widows in Jerusalem, and above all else it was commissioned to take the Christian evangel to the ends of the earth. By contrast the Qumran fellowship was not merely esoteric but introspective, and as history has shown, was unable in the last analysis to augment those spiritual values which it was endeavouring desperately to conserve.

At Qumran the sectaries were under obligation to live together in zeal and brotherly love,[151] and when admitted to the fellowship they were required to bring with them their material wealth as well as their gifts of devotion and intellect.[152] The early Christians were also "of one heart and soul,"[153] and in refusing to recognise personal claims to property had all things in common, which they then distributed according to individual need.[154] But whereas the Qumran novitiates apparently brought only moveable property and personal belongings with them on admission to communal life, the early Christians sold land and houses in order to contribute to the common fund.

Furthermore, this was a voluntary act, and was not in any sense a prerequisite to full fellowship in the Christian community. In addition, the proceeds were devoted to relieving conditions of distress among the poor and needy in the city of Jerusalem, whereas the sectaries by contrast used their resources to provide only for the sick and indigent members of their own fellowship.[155] Finally, the motivation of such activity at Qumran was fully consonant with the esoteric nature of the brotherhood, whereas the early Christians distributed to all without discrimination on the basis of need, thereby exemplifying the poverty, selflessness and generosity of Jesus the Messiah.

The language of the scrolls also exhibits certain points in common with New Testament writings other than the Four Gospels. The ethical significance which St. Paul attached to the term "flesh"[156] occurred in the Qumran literature to designate the frailty and mortality of man.[157] Such is also the case with the concept of "spirit",[158] despite the fact that there are no parallels to such New Testament phrases as "the spirit of the world"[159] or "the spirit of (or from) God."[160] A comparison of the list of vices catalogued by St. Paul as the "works of the flesh"[161] with what the sectaries regarded as the product of the interaction between the spirit of perversity[162] and the individual human personality shows that both the brotherhood and the Apostle were in general agreement concerning the functioning of unregenerate human nature. Again, the hymns of the sectaries often contained the thought that works of righteousness could be found only in God,[163] while the *Rule of the Community* recorded that justification was a Divine prerogative, and was dispensed in accordance with the ethical character of the Deity.[164]

A personal faith in the Righteous Teacher was interpreted in the Habakkuk commentary[165] as a means of salvation from the penal death of the ungodly and those who did not follow the precepts of the Torah, a dictum which has something in common with the doctrine of justification by faith, so characteristic of Pauline thought.[166] It should be observed, however, that the Qumran concept of justification bears little relationship to the concept of a living personal union with Jesus Christ on the basis of confession and faith. Furthermore, whereas the sectaries thought of sanctification as a process to be completed by an act of Divine grace at the final Judgment, St. Paul envisaged it as a continuous refining and deepening of personal spirituality based on justification by faith, and operating at all stages under the direct control of the Holy Spirit.

As might be expected, the Epistle of James, which may be taken broadly as representing the standpoint of Jews converted to Christianity through the influence of the Judaean church rather than through the ministrations of St. Paul, contains parallels in thought and phraseology to the sectarian documents. The concept of "temptation" or "trial"[167] was familiar to the Qumran brotherhood,[168] and the reward of a "crown of life" for the Christian[169] had its counterpart among the sectaries in the glorious diadem and beautiful robe.[170] Some scholars have assumed that the citation which speaks of "the spirit which dwells in man lusting to envy"[171] may have been derived from the Qumran literature, with its emphasis upon the spirit of perversity,[172] and that these writings may perhaps be the "scripture" to which James referred, since the quotation does not actually occur in the Old Testament.[173] Inasmuch as Jude[174] mentioned extra-canonical writings, it is possible that James also followed the same practice in this particular instance.

As a result of the Qumran discoveries it is now no longer necessary to assign the Second Epistle of Peter to a date in the middle of the second century A.D., as has long been maintained by critical scholars.[175] The closeness of its phraseology and thought to that of the Essenes and similar sects which flourished at the beginning of the Christian era indicates quite clearly that the Epistle proceeded strictly from a Palestinian Jewish milieu. Indeed, the emphasis upon the true way, light in the midst of darkness, brotherly love, true and false teachers, and the destruction of the world by fire, is distinctly reminiscent of the Qumran writings, and shows little if any contact with Hellenistic thought.

In the light of the foregoing discussion it will be evident that a great deal of caution must be exercised when undertaking a comparison of early Christian thought and practice with that which obtained among the Qumran sectaries.[176] Even more reserve is required before assigning characteristic Christian institutions to Essene or similar origins in view of the common cultural and religious traditions upon which each drew. For any who may be disturbed about the implications of the Qumran discoveries for the Christian faith, it must be remembered that Christianity is the fulfilment of an historic faith which was rooted in the Old Testament.[177] As Cross has pointed out,

"It is not the idea of redemption through suffering but the "event" of the crucifixion understood as the atoning work of God that distinguishes Christianity. It is not the doctrine of resurrection but faith in the resurrection of Jesus as an eschatological event which forms the basis of the Christian decision of faith. It is not faith that a Messiah will come that gives Christianity its special character, but the assurance that Jesus rules as the Messiah who has come and will come ... The Christian faith is distinguished from the ancient faith which brought it to birth in its knowledge of a new act of God's love, the revelation of His love in Jesus' particular life and death and resurrection."[178]

Some observations by a Jewish scholar, Samuel Sandmel,[179] may well be considered also at this juncture. He has maintained that there is absolutely no evidence which would link early Christianity with the Dead Sea community, holding that any alleged connections between Essene beliefs and Christian teachings are based on speculation and the discovery of parallel forms in the sectarian manuscripts and the New Testament. Where the two ideologies overlap is in that precise area which is the common property of all forms of Judaism, including that from which Christianity itself grew. In short, he has argued that while the scrolls are useful historically in furnishing additional information about Judaism as it obtained in the immediate pre-Christian period, their importance for the origin of Christianity has been greatly exaggerated over the years.

PLATE 1. A scene depicting the gathering and splitting of papyrus for paper making.

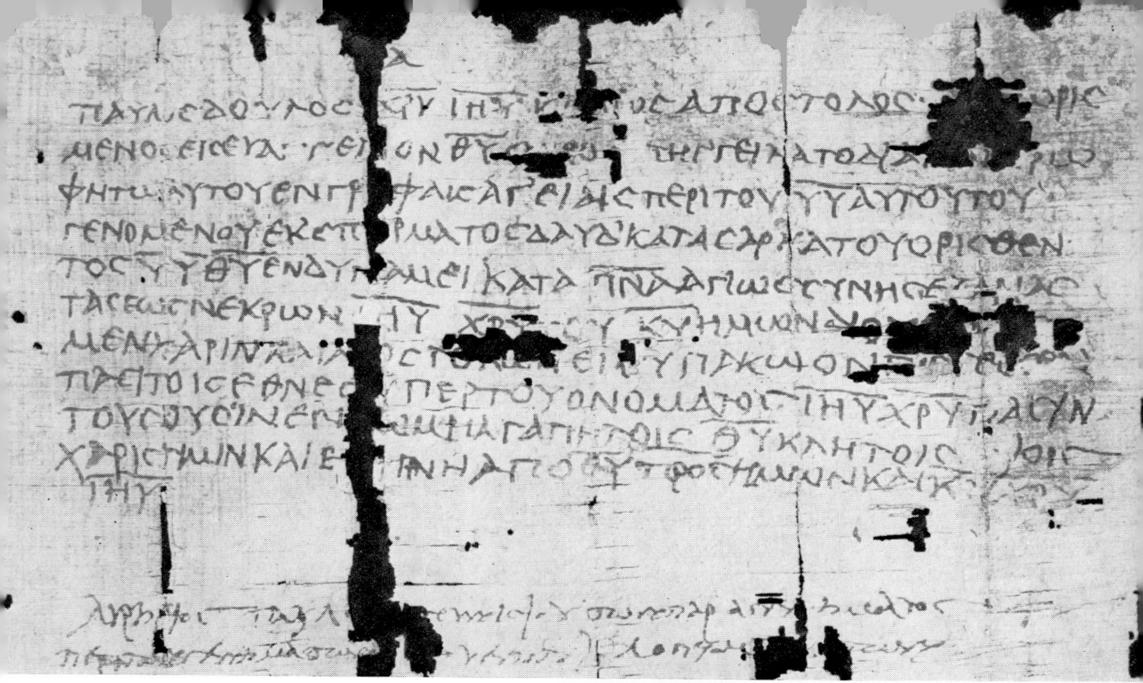

PLATE 2. A papyrus fragment containing the opening lines of the Epistle to the Romans.

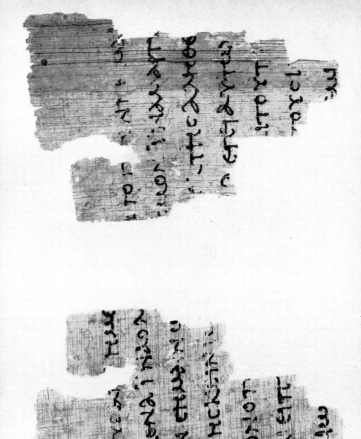

PLATE 3:
*A fragment of
the Fourth
Gospel,
Papyrus
Rylands Gk. 457.*

PLATE 4. Marble bust of Tiberius as a young man.

PLATE 5. A statue of Christ as the Good Shepherd. About the third century A.D.

PLATE 6 APAM(?)

PLATE 8. *Bronze coins from the period of Herod Agrippa I.*

PLATE 7. *The synagogue inscription of Theodotus.*

PLATE 9. *A Greek inscription from Thessalonica, naming Politarchs and other civic officials.*

Chapter VII

NAG HAMMADI AND THE GOSPELS

A SHORT time before the Dead Sea scrolls were discovered in 1947, a group of Egyptian peasants accidentally stumbled upon an entire library of papyrus documents located some thirty miles north of Luxor, in the region of Nag Hammadi near el-Qasr es-Sayyad, the ancient Sheneset-Chenoboskion. The manuscripts were written on papyrus in Coptic of the Sahidic dialect, and many of them had been wrapped in separate leather coverings before being placed together in a large sealed jar, making for an excellent state of preservation. Thirteen separate codices were found to contain forty-eight treatises, including some duplicate copies, which must have amounted originally to about one thousand pages.[1] Specialists in Coptic philology dated the codices in the late third and early fourth centuries A.D., and established the fact that they had in the main been translated from Greek originals.

At the time the documents were discovered the peasants apparently divided them up into several lots,[2] and nearly four years elapsed before they were all acquired for the Coptic museum in Cairo in 1950. After preliminary study the scholars came to the conclusion that the manuscripts constituted the remains of a library belonging to a religious community which had perhaps been established early in the fourth century A.D. That it was not orthodox in nature was evident from the fact that other than Christian scriptures had been used by the group. The close relationship between the Nag Hammadi manuscripts and other kinds of heretical literature circulating during the second, third and fourth centuries A.D. furnished clear indications as to the nature of the religious brotherhood. Its members were quite obviously Gnostics, a term derived from a Greek word implying ability to attain to knowledge. It is known from a variety of sources that there were various kinds of Gnostics during the first few centuries of the Christian era, and one important aspect of the Nag Hammadi discoveries is that certain of the manuscripts represent one of the purest strains of this kind of teaching. Taken together, the scrolls and fragments comprised a wide variety of ancient literature, and this corpus is of particular significance because prior to 1946 only a very few original Gnostic documents were extant.

A number of the manuscripts are mystical in nature, and deal with alleged revelations given to certain Old Testament figures, notably Seth, son of Adam.[3] Of a more Christian character were a group of secret writings purporting to record the discussions which took place between Christ and His disciples just previous to the ascension into heaven.[4] There are also a number of epistles, the more important being the *Epistle of Philip to Peter* and the *Epistle of Eugnostos the Blessed*, along with other diverse compositions.

Publication of this new material took place with disappointing slowness when compared with the way in which the principal Qumran documents were made available to the world of scholarship, but in 1956 a photostatic copy of the *Gospel According to Thomas* was published, and later that year it was followed by an edition of the *Gospel of Truth* in French, German and English. In 1959 a group of scholars translated the *Gospel According to Thomas*, but did not comment on the text at that time[5]. When the discovery of the manuscripts was announced by a group of European scholars, it was stated that this *Gospel* contained material of importance for the literary study of the New Testament and that it included certain sayings of Jesus previously unknown.[6]

It should be stated at this juncture that in point of fact the work cannot be regarded as a "Gospel" in the generally accepted sense. It claims to be a record of the secret sayings spoken by the living Jesus as recorded by Didymus Judas Thomas. Since the book was written about the third century A.D. the author was obviously not the Apostle Thomas. The material contained in this document consisted of just over one hundred short sayings, dialogues and parables, set down in a continuous textual form without any particular arrangement and omitting all reference to the life and work of Christ.[7] Many of the sayings merely commenced with "Jesus said" or "He said", while at other times they were provoked by a question from one or other of the disciples.

There is close agreement between certain sayings in the *Gospel According to Thomas* and some contained in a few celebrated Egyptian documents discovered by Grenfell and Hunt in 1897 and 1903. These were the Oxyrhynchus papyri, and consisted of three Greek fragments containing sixteen sayings of Jesus,[8] all of which occur in the *Gospel According to Thomas* with some variation in matters of detail. The nature of this correspondence can be illustrated by the following citation:

> "Jesus said: If those who lead you say to you:
> 'See, the Kingdom is in Heaven',
> Then the birds of the heaven will precede you . . .[9]
> If they say to you: 'It is in the sea,'
> then the fish will precede you."[10]

Perhaps the most familiar of the Oxyrhynchus sayings is found in the *Gospel According to Thomas* as follows:

> "Cleave a (piece of) wood, I am there;
> lift up the stone and you will find me there."[11]

which appeared in reverse order in the Oxyrhynchus fragments. From textual variations it is possible to state that the Coptic version was revised after being translated from the Greek, and that both appeared to have drawn in the first instance upon the same collection of the words of Jesus.

Before the discovery of this Coptic *Gospel According to Thomas*, two rather contradictory reports of such material had been transmitted from early Christian times. The first was to the effect that from the Apostolic period there were in existence certain versions of a *Gospel of Thomas* which purported to be a collection of stories about the boyhood days of Jesus.[12] From such citations of this work as have survived it appears that, while some of the incidents narrated in this *Gospel* were of a decidedly fanciful nature, the bulk of the composition contained little if anything that the early Church could have rejected as heretical.

Alongside these references to a *Gospel of Thomas* were others which occurred in the writings of the Early Fathers, and spoke in a rather disparaging manner of a literary work associated with the Apostle but which in reality was commonly attributed to the work of heretical groups. Thus Origen, in the first of the *Homilies on Luke* (*c.* A.D. 246), mentioned it in the comment:

"I know a certain *Gospel* which is called 'according to Thomas', and one 'according to Matthias', and several others we have read."[13]

In his *Church History*, Eusebius (*c.* A.D. 260–340) recorded that there were in circulation in his day:

". . . writings which are put forward by heretics under the name of apostles containing Gospels such as those of Peter, and Thomas, and Matthias, and some others besides . . ."[14]

In process of writing about the Naasene sect, Hippolytus (*c.* A.D. 170–236) mentioned a gospel associated with the name of Thomas:

"And concerning this (nature) they hand down an explicit passage, occurring in the Gospel inscribed according to Thomas, expressing themselves thus; 'He who seeks me will find me in children from seven years old; for there concealed, I shall in the fourteenth age be made manifest.' This, however, is not (the teaching) of Christ, but of Hippocrates, who uses these words: 'A child of seven years is half of a father" . . ."[15]

This citation may in fact reflect one of the *logia* in the Coptic *Gospel According to Thomas*, which reads as follows:

"Jesus said: The man old in days will not hesitate to ask a little child of seven days about the place of Life, and he will live."[16]

Other patristic writers who mentioned a *Gospel of Thomas* included Cyril of Jerusalem, who attributed it to a disciple of Manes and warned all true believers against it.[17]

With the recovery of the Coptic manuscripts it has now become evident that the two traditions in the early Church relating to a gospel associated with Thomas were to entirely different and separate works, each of which bore the name of the Apostle. The account of the childhood of Jesus is not particularly heretical in content and has no connection with Gnostic sects. On the other hand, the Coptic *Gospel According to Thomas* is a specific Gnostic product and consists wholly of sayings or dialogue rather than narrative passages.

On examination the material in the newly-discovered

Coptic Gospel falls into two rough classes, consisting of
sections parallel to the New Testament Gospels, and
logia with a definite Gnostic background of doctrine.
Somewhat less than half of the material in the *Gospel
According to Thomas* will be familiar to readers of the New
Testament, though it should be noted that such parallels
as there are seldom consist of the word-for-word agreement of the kind commonly found in the first three
Gospels. Those *logia* which exhibit only partial parallels
with the canonical Gospels frequently commence in a
familiar manner and subsequently proceed to Gnostic
doctrine and terminology. A surprising characteristic of
the Coptic *Gospel* is the absence of close parallels to the
Fourth Gospel. There are only four passages[18] which can
be regarded as in any sense similar to Johannine
material. This circumstance is somewhat unusual
because, according to papyrus discoveries, the Fourth
Gospel was in circulation in Egypt during the second
century A.D., and in consequence must presumably have
been known to the community which produced the
Gospel According to Thomas. Equally curious is the fact
that of the thirty or so *logia* which include phrases
reminiscent of St. Mark, there are only about twelve
fairly close parallels, and even here it is difficult to be
sure that they are nearer to the Markan version than
that of Matthew or Luke.[19]

Most readers will be interested in the extent to which
the Coptic *Gospel* contains hitherto unknown and
authentic sayings of Christ. Those *logia* which are of a
specifically Gnostic character can be dismissed immediately, since Jesus was not a Gnostic. Again, those
sayings which reflect the general tenor of utterances in
the Synoptic Gospels but with certain differences in
detail can also be excluded, since they are obviously
later developments. Of the few which remain, some can
be eliminated on grounds such as historical improb-

ability,[20] while others may be suspect because of diffi-culties in interpretation.[21] It should be noted, however, that ease of interpretation is not necessarily a criterion of authenticity in the Coptic *Gospel*, as, indeed, in any other religious writing. Nevertheless, some agreement regard-ing interpretation is desirable as a prerequisite to evaluating the genuineness of some *logia*.

On this basis it would appear probable that certain sayings reflect the same kind of tradition as that which preserved the *logion* quoted by St. Paul, "It is more blessed to give than to receive."[22] One such utterance stressed the responsibilities to be exercised by the believer in respect of his fellow:

"Jesus said: Love thy brother as thy soul, guard him as the apple of thine eye."[23]

Another, which has much in common with the Gospel statement about the character of true discipleship reads:

"Jesus said: Whoever is near to me is near to the fire, and whoever is far from me is far from the King-dom."[24]

Among the *logia* of this Coptic *Gospel* is a saying which reflected the sinlessness characteristic of the self-estimate of Christ,[25] and which reads as follows:

"They said (to Him): Come and let us pray today and let us fast. Jesus said: Which then is the sin that I have committed, or in what have I been van-quished?"[26]

Perhaps a new saying can also be added to the Beatitudes[27] with the preservation of the utterance:

"Blessed is the man who has suffered: he has found the Life"[28] where the concept of suffering as integral to the process of spiritual maturity is in harmony with the emphasis of Scripture generally.

In order to appreciate the true nature of the Coptic document, a few comments regarding the Gnostics themselves would seem to be appropriate. As their name implies, they were more concerned with attaining to superior knowledge[29] than in practising faith, penitence and love. While many of them claimed some vague relationship to Christianity, they were never members of the Christian Church in the strictest sense. They refused to be satisfied with anything less than a completely intellectual religion, and while they often professed great respect for Christ they were never entirely committed to Him.[30] Some, indeed, claimed to have received secret traditions from the Apostles, and these they held in great esteem, boasting that they were of a more exalted kind than those circulating in the Church.

Members of the Gnostic sects were chiefly concerned with two problems. The first raised the question as to how an infinite spiritual deity could be connected with a finite and material world. The second enquired as to the origin and nature of evil. Some Gnostics taught that the Creator of the world, whom they identified with the God of the Old Testament, was an inferior evil being, while others ascribed the work of creation generally to the activities of angels or other less exalted creatures.[31] They also held that man belonged spiritually to the higher realm of existence, but because he was imprisoned in a material, and therefore evil, body he was powerless to realise his true destiny. Christ came to earth in human form so as to pioneer for mankind the way to heaven, and break for all time the dominance of the material world.[32]

Such were the basic beliefs of the religious community whose fragmentary library was so unexpectedly dis-

covered at Chenoboskion, and it is in the light of these
tenets that the contents of the *Gospel According to Thomas*
must be assessed. The Gnostic attitude of distaste for the
world was expressed in a saying which maintained that
the person who has come to understand the true nature
of the physical universe realises that it is at best a paltry,
dead thing. Yet in this very estimate of the values inherent in physical phenomena he has demonstrated that
by thought he has overcome the world.[33] No doubt this
concept of non-involvement in the maze of worldly living
prompted the Coptic *Gospel* to record that Jesus taught
His followers to be "passers-by" in the world.[34]

The sense of self-contradiction and internal tension
which the Gnostics attributed to man through being
created from a fusion of superior and inferior elements
was reflected in the following rather cryptic saying:

> "Jesus said: If the flesh has come into existence
> because of (the) Spirit, it is a marvel; but if (the)
> Spirit (has come into existence) because of the body
> it is a marvel of marvels."[35]

Prominent in the *Gospel According to Thomas* was the
typical Gnostic emphasis upon hidden, esoteric knowledge about the Deity, the universe and other aspects of
existence.[36] In consequence, several of the sayings
stressed self-knowledge as a means of understanding the
meaning of existence, as in the following citation:

> "Jesus said: . . . If you (will) know yourselves, then
> you will be known and you will know that you are the
> sons of the Living Father. But if you do not know
> yourselves, then you are in poverty and you are
> poverty."[37]

And again,

> "Jesus said: Whoever knows the All but fails (to
> know) himself lacks everything."[38]

A number of "hard sayings" of a rather curious variety also occur in the Coptic *Gospel*. One of these is as follows:

> "Blessed is the lion which the man eats and the lion will become man; and cursed is the man whom the lion eats and the lion will become man."[39]

Other material from Nag Hammadi may perhaps furnish a key to the "spiritual" analogy of this and similar passages, but until such an eventuality occurs the text must be regarded as obscure at the best. Indeed, the question might well be raised in the mind of the reader as to exactly what superior knowledge was contained in material of this kind, and the extent to which it was deemed worthy of preservation for posterity.

The characteristic Gnostic attitude towards sex as something intrinsically evil, and therefore to be repudiated in favour of the ascetic ideal, is reflected in certain of these "previously unknown" sayings of Christ. One of the more significant of this group recorded Peter objecting strenuously to Mary remaining among the band of disciples, because in his view women were unworthy to share in such an exalted way of life. To this Jesus replied:

> "See, I shall lead her, so that I will make her male, that she too may become a living spirit, resembling you males."[40]

The *Gospel According to Thomas* concluded at this point with the observation that every woman who makes herself male will enter the kingdom of Heaven. Whatever else may be said about this extraordinary aphorism, it is certainly entirely opposed in spirit to the attitude of Christ towards women generally.

Other sayings in the Coptic *Gospel* also expressed concepts which are far from being in agreement with the normal theme of the words of Jesus as recorded in the New Testament. One such utterance, for example, stated that the one who gives alms does his own spirit an injury, while those who pray will be condemned, and the pious who fast merely lay themselves open to future sin.[41]

Any estimate of the significance of this newly-recovered Coptic source, and indeed of other material from the same location, must of necessity take cognisance of the essential natures of Gnosticism and Christianity respectively. The Nag Hammadi treatises constitute a substantial addition to extant Gnostic literature, and indicate that the way in which the early Christian writers depicted the various facets of Gnosticism was substantially correct. On the basis of this new collection of sources it is now possible to reconstruct the Gnostic system with a high degree of confidence; to relate it more consistently to its Greek and oriental background, and to estimate its impact upon both Judaism and early Christianity.

As far as the latter is concerned, the reader will doubtless already have come to the conclusion that, while the Coptic *Gospel* exhibits some familiarity with the Synoptic tradition, it has in fact very little of abiding spiritual or moral value to offer. It cannot be regarded as one of the sources of our present Gospels, and it is difficult to see how it can in any way affect the doctrines implicit in the sayings of Christ to any noticeable extent. The work is of importance, however, in throwing light on the validity of the claims made by certain liberal scholars, notably Rudolph Bultmann,[42] that the New Testament writers depended for their material to a large extent upon Gnostic myths, particularly in their understanding of the person and work of Christ.[43]

The manuscript sources have already demonstrated in this connection that there are far fewer traces of Gnosticism in the New Testament than had been supposed previously. It is clear that the description of the perfect man, Adam, given in the *Apocryphon of John,* has no relationship whatever to the "type of him who was to come,"[44] nor do the sources generally support the theory advanced by Bultmann concerning a pre-Christian redeemer myth, since they obviously envisaged Jesus appearing "in the flesh" as a real person and not as a mythical entity.

While the *Gospel According to Thomas* cannot in any sense be considered as a "fifth gospel", it is of very great importance for quite a different reason. Along with the other writings from the monastic community at Nag Hammadi, it is an invaluable witness to the nature of a religious movement with which early Christianity came into contact, and which still survives to some extent under different forms in the modern world.[45] So far from undermining the Christian faith, the recently-discovered Coptic *Gospel* has actually rendered it an indirect service by demonstrating quite convincingly that there is no valid reason for questioning the genuine nature of the sayings of Jesus as recorded in the Four Gospels. Above everything else they have shown that behind the literary tradition of the Evangelists stands a Person whose words have been transmitted in substantially unchanged form by responsible New Testament authors.

NOTES TO CHAPTERS

Chapter I

1. F. Kenyon, *The Bible and Archaeology* (1949), p. 38. These statues were similar to those uncovered by Paul Emile Botta at Khorsabad in 1844. Cf. S. Lloyd, *Foundations in the Dust* (1949), p. 111 seq.; C. W. Ceram, *Gods, Graves and Scholars* (1951), pp. 214 seq., 254 seq.

2. C. L. Woolley, *Ur of the Chaldees* (1950), p. 27 seq.

3. For a brief account *vide* A. Parrot, *Mari, une ville perdue* (1935).

4. A popular description of the work at Nuzu has been furnished by E. Chiera, *They Wrote on Clay* (1939).

5. S. A. B. Mercer, *The Tell el-Amarna Tablets* (1939), 2 vols.

6. B. P. Grenfell and A. S. Hunt, *Sayings of Our Lord* (1897); *LAP*, p. 323.

7. As Albright, *AP*, p. 239 has indicated, the impact of New Testament archaeology has been correspondingly less than was the case with similar work in the Old Testament field because Graeco-Roman history and culture were much more familiar than the earlier phases of Near Eastern history.

8. G. A. Barton, *Archaeology and the Bible* (1937), p. 208 f. Cf. J. H. Breasted, *The Conquest of Civilisation* (1938), p. 156.

9. F. A. Banks, *Coins of Bible Days* (1955), p. 21.

10. For a description of early numismatic discoveries *in loco* cf. *RB* (1954), LXI, p. 230 f.

11.   Cf. A. Kindler, *Antiquity and Survival* (1957), II,
       p. 225 f.

12.   Luke 15:8 f.

13.   Matt. 17:24. It was worth approximately twice as
       much as the *drachma*.

14.   Matt. 17:27. This was the *stater*, worth about four
       times as much as the *drachma*.

15.   Matt. 18:24, 25:15 ff. Talents of gold were also in
       use at this time.

16.   Luke 19:13 f.

17.   Matt. 18:28, 20:2, 9 f, 13 *et al*.

18.   Matt. 5:26.

19.   Matt. 10:29, Luke 12:6. This is the "farthing"
       of the English versions.

20.   Mark 12:42. Originally a non-Roman coin. For a
       recent estimate of the value of the foregoing coins
       cf. G. A. Barrois, *The Interpreter's Bible* (1952), I,
       p. 157 f.

21.   Matt. 22:19 ff. The superscription read, TI.
       CAESAR DIVI AVG. F. AVGVSTVS, (*Tiberius
       Caesar, Augustus, son of Divine Augustus*) and on the
       reverse side PONTIF. MAXIM. (*Pontifex
       Maximus*).

22.   Cf. Mark 12:41 ff.; Luke 12:58 f.

23.   Cf. *AP*, p. 172.

24.   W. F. Albright, *Recent Discoveries in Bible Lands*
       (1955), p. 112.

25.   Acts 6:9.

26.   In the ancient Near East bricks and other con-
       structional materials were frequently stamped
       with the name of the ruler in whose reign the
       building was erected.

27.   *I.e., Legio Decima Fretensis*. The adjective Fretensis
       commemorated some great event, perhaps the

batttle near the straits between Italy and Sicily in
36 B.C. under Octavian.

28. "Sacred to the memory of L. Magnius Felix, a
soldier of the tenth legion, the Fretensis, who was
an orderly to the tribune, served eighteen years,
and died aged thirty-nine." A. C. Bouquet,
Everyday Life in New Testament Times (1956), p. 26.

29. *WBA*, pl. 187.

30. *WBA*, pl. 188.

31. A. Parrot, *Le Musée du Louvre et la Bible* (1957),
p. 139 f. There may be a reference to this queen
in the Qumran Copper Scroll. Cf. J. M. Allegro,
The Treasure of the Copper Scroll (1960), pp. 42 f,
Item 28, 150 n 136.

32. Cf. *WBA*, pl. 189.

33. *AP*, p. 159.

34. *AP*, p. 160 and pl. 26.

35. E. L. Sukenik, *AJA* (1947), LI, p. 351 seq. Cf. A.
Parrot, *Golgotha and the Church of the Holy Sepulchre*
(1957), p. 113 seq.

36. An abbreviation for Mattathias.

37. According to Sukenik these are typical Greek
funerary exclamations of woe or misfortune. B.
Gustafsson, *NTS* (1957), III, p. 65 seq. has interpreted the phrase *Iesou Iou* as "Jesus help!", *i.e.*, a
prayer addressed to Christ as the living risen Lord,
testifying to the early Christian belief in the
resurrection of Jesus.

38. Acts 1:23.

39. Acts 15:22.

40. *Cyperus papyrus L.*, also designated *Papyrus anti-
quorum* Willd., the Egyptian bulrush. H. N. and
A. L. Moldenke, *Plants of the Bible* (1952), pp. 92 ff.

41. P. E. Newberry, *Egypt as a Field for Anthropological
Research* (1925), pp. 435 ff.

42. For the papyrus as an architectural ornament cf. H. Frankfort, *Ancient Egyptian Religion* (1961), pp. 151, 154.

43. *LAP*, pl. 127.

44. F. G. Kenyon, *The Palaeography of Greek Papyri* (1899), p. 14. Pliny (*Hist. Nat.* XIII, 13) questioned the statement by the Roman antiquarian Varro (*c.* 116–27 B.C.) that papyrus was first used as writing material in the time of Alexander the Great.

45. For the presence of third century B.C. papyrus fragments at Dura-Europos in Mesopotamia cf. C. B. Welles, *Münchener Beiträge zur Papyrusforschung und antiken Rechtsgeschichte* (1934), XIX, p. 379 seq.

46. *Hist. Nat.* XIII. 11 f.

47. The longest extant roll is the Harris papyrus from the reign of Rameses II, measuring seventeen inches in height and one hundred and thirty three feet in length. *ARE*, IV. Sect. 151 seq.

48. A roll inscribed on the *recto* and *verso* is known as an *opisthograph*. Cf. Rev. 5:1.

49. The *kalamos* of 3 John v. 13.

50. The *melan* of 2 Cor. 3:3; 2 John v. 12; 3 John v. 13.

51. One was made from lampblack, gum and water, the other from nutgalls, vitriol and water. The latter turned a dark brown in process of time. Cf. W. H. P. Hatch, *The Principal Uncial Manuscripts of the New Testament* (1939), pp. 13 ff.

52. Cf. Rev. 22:18 f. The Greek is the diminutive of *biblos*, a term derived from the pith of the papyrus stalk.

53. 2 Tim. 4:13.

54. The Latin *caudex*, meaning "tree trunk", was used of blocks of wood split up into leaves or tablets

which were then often covered with wax and written upon. These were the "large tablets" of Isaiah 8:1, 30:8; Luke 1:63. Cf. G. Milligan, *The New Testament and Its Transmission* (1932), p. 15.

55. Cf. C. C. McCown, *BA* (1943), VI, No. 1, p. 21 seq.

56. C. H. Roberts, *An Unpublished Fragment of the Fourth Gospel in the John Rylands Library* (1935). The Bodmer Papyrus containing the Gospels of Luke and John is another ancient New Testament manuscript, dated A. D. 175–225. Cf. V. Martin and R. Kasser, *Papyrus Bodmer* XIV–XV: *Évangiles de Luc et Jean*. Tomes I–II (1961); B. M. Metzger, *ET* (1962), LXXIII, pp. 201 ff.; F. V. Filson, *BA* (1962), XXV, No. 2, p. 50 seq.

57. H. A. Sanders, *A Third Century Papyrus Codex of the Epistles of Paul* (1935).

58. F. G. Kenyon, *The Chester Beatty Biblical Papyri*, Fasc. III. Text 1934; Suppl. Text 1936; Suppl. Plates 1937.

59. U. Wilcken, *Archiv für Papyrusforschung* (1935), XI, p. 113.

60. Thus the prophecies of Jeremiah were probably written upon a leather roll (cf. Jer. 36:4,23), as was the case with many of the Dead Sea scrolls. The Talmud (*Maccoth.* 5) preserved an ancient tradition that the Mosaic Torah was written upon the hides of cattle. According to Josephus (*AJ.* XII, 2, 11), the Pentateuchal manuscript from which the LXX was translated was written upon leather. Cf. the *Letter of Aristeas*, iii, 176.

61. Parchment was specially processed so as to be able to receive writing on both sides, whereas vellum was made from calfskins only. G. Peignot, *Essai sur l'histoire du parchemin et du vélin* (1812), p. 28.

62. *Anthropos* to ANC or ANOC.

63. *Stauros* to CTC, CPC or CTPC.

64. Tischendorf described his dramatic discovery in
     *Codex Sinaiticus, the Ancient Biblical Manuscript now
     in the British Museum, Tischendorf's Story and Argu-
     ment Related by Himself* (1934 ed.), p. 23 f. The
     manuscript is dated *c.* A.D. 350, and is one of the
     principal New Testament manuscripts.

65. Of about the same age as Codex Sinaiticus, it has
     been in the Vatican Library for many centuries.
     It contains almost the entire Greek Bible.

66. F. G. Kenyon, *Handbook to the Textual Criticism of
     the New Testament* (1912), p. 124.

67. The scribe Tertius is mentioned in Rom. 16:22.

68. Eg., 2 Thess. 3:17.

69. Gal. 6:11.

70. J. Baikie, *Egyptian Papyri and Papyrus Hunting*
     (1925), p. 16.

71. B. P. Grenfell, A. S. Hunt and D. G. Hogarth,
     Fayum Towns and Their Papyri (1900).

72. In some localities in Egypt the sun-deity Re was
     known as Sobek-Re, the crocodile-god.

73. B. P. Grenfell, L. W. Drexel and A. S. Hunt, *New
     Sayings of Jesus and a Fragment of a Lost Gospel* (1904).

74. J. H. Moulton, *Grammar of New Testament Greek*
     (1908), I, Prolegomena, p. 3.

75. Cf. 2 Cor. 3:2.

76. G. Milligan, *Here and There Among the Papyri* (1922),
     p. 33 f.

77. Cf. 1 Cor. 15:31.

78. Giessen papyri I, No. 17; Milligan, *Here and
     There Among the Papyri*, p. 98.

79. Identified with Osiris in the Greek period.

80. A village in the Fayyum, perhaps where the
     writer originally lived.

81. G. Milligan, *Selections From the Greek Papyri* (1910), p. 93 f.

82. Cf. A. S. Hunt and C. C. Edgar, *Select Papyri* (Loeb Classical Library, 1932–34), 2 vols.; F. J. Goodspeed and E. C. Colwell, *A Greek Papyrus Reader* (1935).

83. R. Rothe, *Zur Dogmatik* (1863), p. 238, cited by J. H. Moulton and G. Milligan, *The Vocabulary of the Greek Testament* (1930), p. xi.

84. G. Milligan, *The New Testament Documents, their Origin and Early History* (1913), p. 93.

85. Gal. 6-11.

86. This fact is of help in delineating the limits of stylistic criticism.

Chapter II

1. Cf. F. M. Abel, *Géographie de la Palestine* (1938), II, p. 222 seq.

2. R. Beauvery, *RB* (1957), LXIV, p. 72 f.

3. 1 Sam. 16:4 seq.; Matt. 2:1; Luke 2:4.

4. Josephus, *WJ*, I, 21, 4, commented, "There was not any place of his kingdom fit for the purpose, that was permitted to be without somewhat that was for Caesar's honour."

5. *WJ*, I, 13, 8; I, 21, 10: *AJ*, XIV, 13, 9.

6. *WJ*, I, 33, 9; *AJ*, XVII, 8, 3.

7. *Sebastos* was the Greek form of the Latin title "Augustus".

8. *WBA*, pl. 160.

9. Cf. G. A. Reisner, C. S. Fisher and D. G. Lyon, *Harvard Excavations at Samaria* 1908–1910 (1924), I, pp. 48 ff.; J. W. Crowfoot, K. M. Kenyon and E. L. Sukenik, *The Buildings At Samaria* (1942), p. 123 seq.

10. For an aerial view of the site *vide WBA*, pl. 161.
    Cf. C. T. Fritsch and I. Ben-Dor, *BA* (1961),
    XXIV, No. 2, p. 50.

11. *WBA*, pl. 78, 79.

12. *AP*, p. 154 f.; cf. K. M. Kenyon, *Illustrated London
    News*, April 14th., 1962, pp. 578 ff.

13. *WJ*, V, 4, 4.

14. *WJ*, V, 5, 8.

15. Acts 21:27 seq.

16. *WBA*, pl. 166.; L-H. Vincent, *Jérusalem de l'Ancien
    Testament* (1954), I, p. 207 f. and pl. xliv.

17. John 19:13. Cf. *AP*, p. 245.; M. Burrows, *BA*
    (1938), I, No. 3, p. 17 f.

18. Cf. L-H. Vincent, *RB* (1952), LIX, p. 513 f.

19. A. Parrot, *The Temple of Jerusalem* (1957), p. 76
    seq.

20. These vaults are popularly known as "Solomon's
    stables".

21. *LAP*, pl. 110. It was here that the Jews lamented
    the destruction of the Temple in subsequent
    centuries.

22. These retaining walls survived the overthrow of
    the Temple buildings under Titus in A.D. 70.
    Cf. Mark 13:2.

23. Cf. the "pinnacle" of Matt. 4:5.; Luke 4:9.;
    AJ, XV, 11, 5.

24. John 10:23; Acts 3:11, 5:12.

25. *AJ*, XX, 9, 7.

26. Mark 11:15 f.

27. *WJ*, V, 5, 25. Cf. *WJ*, VI, 2, 4; *AJ*, XV, 11, 5.

28. Cf. Matt. 23:16.

29. *Hist.* V, 8. Cf. Mark 13:1.

30. *Sukkah.* V, 2.

31. Cf. John 2:1 seq.

32. Cf. Matt. 8:5, 17:24; Mark 2:1, 9:33; Luke 4:23, 7:1. For various identifications of the site cf. S. L. Caiger, *Archaeology and the New Testament* (1948), p. 83.

33. Cf. H. Kohl and C. Watzinger, *Antike Synagogen in Galiläa* (1916), p. 4 seq.; E. L. Sukenik, *Ancient Synagogues in Palestine and Greece* (1934), p. 7 seq.

34. L. Waterman, *Preliminary Report of the University of Michigan Excavations at Sepphoris, Palestine, in 1931* (1937), p. 28 f.

35. Josh. 6:26.

36. 1 Kgs. 16:34. Cf. *AP*, p. 33 f. No clear archaeological evidence of this period has been found.

37. K. M. Kenyon, *Digging Up Jericho* (1957), p. 263.

38. The mound representing Old Testament Jericho is now known as Kom el-Sultan.

39. Traditionally identified with the spring whose waters were "cured" by Elisha. 2 Kgs. 2:19 seq. For a study of the settlements in the Jericho region during the Roman period cf. L. Mowry, *BA* (1952) XV, No. 2, p. 26 seq.

40. *AJ*, XVI, 5, 2., *WJ*, I, 21, 4.

41. *AJ*, XVII, 6, 3.

42. *AJ*, XVII, 8, 2., *WJ*, I, 33, 8.

43. Cp. Luke 10:30.

CHAPTER III

1. Luke 2:1. It was probably on account of Herod's age and illness that the order for the census was issued. Cf. A. Plummer, *The Gospel According to St. Luke* (International Critical Commentary, 1901), p. 49.

2. Luke 2:1 f.

3. Matt. 2:1.

4. W. M. Ramsay, *Was Christ Born at Bethlehem?*
    (1898), p. 123 f. The census recorded in Luke is to
    be distinguished from a later one (A.D. 6)
    mentioned in Acts 5:37.

5. *Stromateis* I, 21, 147.

6. Cf. A. T. Robertson, *Luke the Historian in the Light
    of Research* (1920), pp. 123 ff.

7. The facsimile of the edict and the restored Greek
    text are contained in A. Deissmann, *Light From the
    Ancient East* (1910), p. 268 f. and pl. 42.

8. If Mary was actually heir to the family property,
    she would be required to marry within the tribe
    (Num. 27:1 seq.; 36:1 seq.). Joseph was described
    as the "son of Heli" (Luke 3:23), thus apparently
    being considered the legal heir of Mary's father
    in the absence of male offspring. Cf. N. Gelden-
    huys, *Commentary on the Gospel of Luke* (1950), p.
    151 f.

9. E. M. Blaiklock, *Out of the Earth* (1961), p. 17.
    Tausiris, like the Mary of tradition, must have
    been in her late teens when her son was born.

10. G. Milligan, *Selections From the Greek Papyri* (1910),
    p. 81 f.

11. E.g., E. Schürer, *The Jewish People in the Time of
    Jesus Christ* (1890), I, 2, p. 105 seq.

12. Josephus, *AJ*, XVIII, 1, 1, does not, however,
    imply that this was the first census of Quirinius.
    For problems of chronology *vide* A. R. C. Leaney,
    The Gospel According to St. Luke (1958), p. 44 seq.;
    F. F. Bruce, *Twentieth Century Encyclopedia of
    Religious Knowledge* (1955), I, p. 222; *LAP*, p. 219.
    F. M. Heichelheim in T. Frank (Ed.), *An Economic
    Survey of Ancient Rome* (1938), IV, p. 161 has
    suggested that Luke 2:2 should be translated,
    "This census was the first before that under the
    prefectureship of Quirinius in Syria". However,

this is not the meaning conveyed by the Greek text.

13. A. Robertson, *Luke the Historian in the Light of Research*, p. 128.; *BRD*, p. 285 and pl. 1.

14. *BRD*, p. 291. Cf. W. M. Ramsay, *Journal of Roman Studies* (1917), VII, pp. 271 ff.

15. *Adv. Marc.*, IV, 19.

16. *Classical Review* (1927), XLI, p. 151.; M. F. Unger, *Archaeology and the New Testament* (1962), p. 65.

17. F. F. Bruce, *Are the New Testament Documents Reliable?* (1946), p. 85. Cf. *NAD*, p. 538.; H. D. A. Major in H. D. A. Major, T. W. Manson and C. J. Wright, *The Mission and Message of Jesus* (1940), p. 267.

18. Cf. F. G. Kenyon, *Classical Review* (1893), VII, p. 110.; T. Corbishley, *Klio* (1936), XXIX, pp. 81 ff.

19. A. Toynbee, *The Study of History* (1954), VII, p. 298. Cf. C. H. Turner in J. Hastings (Ed.), *A Dictionary of the Bible* (1903), I, p. 404.

20. *LAP*, p. 219.

21. Jer. 41:17.

22. Cf. A. P. Stanley, *Sinai and Palestine* (1885), pp. 163, 529. Perhaps it is the same place as the Mandra of Josephus, *AJ*, X, 9, 5.

23. Cf. 2 Sam. 19:31 seq.

24. *Kataluma*. This should not be translated "inn".

25. *KBA*, p. 361 f.

26. R. W. Hamilton, *The Church of the Nativity, Bethlehem* (1947), p. 91 seq. For a description of the site and its environs *vide* Caiger, *Archaeology and the New Testament*, p. 77 f.

27. Luke 2:22.

28. Matt. 2:16 seq.

29. Cf. *AJ*, XVII, 6, 6.

30. Luke 2:46 seq.

31. Luke 3:23.

32. Mark 6:3.

33. Luke 3:1.

34. Cf. *WJ*, XX, 7, 1.

35. *Corpus Inscriptionorum Graecorum* (1828–77), III, No. 4521.

36. J. M. Creed, *The Gospel According to St. Luke* (1950), p. 309.; *WMTS*, pp. 84 f., 282.

37. John 5:1 seq.

38. *KBA*, p. 392 f.

39. Cf. J. M. Allegro, *The Treasure of the Copper Scroll*, pp. 52 f, Item 56, 165 f. n 282.

40. John 7:10 seq.

41. 2 Kgs. 20:20.

42. Translated in J. B. Pritchard (Ed.), *Ancient Near Eastern Texts Relating to the Old Testament* (1955), p. 321. Cf. *AP*, p. 135.

43. John 9:7.

44. Mark 13:1 f.

45. *WJ*, V, 12, 4; VI, 1, 1.

46. Matt. 26:57; Mark 14:53; Luke 22:54.

47. Luke 23:33.

48. Matt. 27:60; Mark 15:46; Luke 23:53; John 19:41.

49. Greek *Lithostratos*, Hebrew *Gabbatha*. John 19:13.

50. Cf. *AP*, p. 245 and pl. 63.

51. Mark 15:16.

52. *WHAB*, p. 106 f. This view is also maintained by R. P. P. Benoit, *RB* (1952), LIX, p. 531 f.; *KBA*, p. 405 f.

53.   *WJ*, II, 14, 8.

54.   In the time of Hadrian a terrace and a sanctuary dedicated to Venus were erected on the traditional site of Calvary (Eusebius, *Life of Constantine*, III, 26) but Constantine removed this pagan edifice and constructed in its place a magnificent basilica which was dedicated in A.D. 335. For a description of the site by the "Bordeaux Pilgrim" in A.D. 333 cf. A. Stewart (Trans.), *Itinerary From Bordeaux to Jerusalem* (1887), p. 23 f.

55.   *WHAB*, pl. XVIIc

56.   *KBA*, Map XVIII.

57.   *AP*, p. 154 f.; *WHAB*, p. 107.

58.   For a survey of legendary accretions concerning Calvary cf. J. Jeremias, *Golgotha* (1926), p. 30 seq.

59.   Cf. R. Dussaud, *Les monuments palestiniens et judaïques* (1912), pp. 47, 58, 88.

60.   L-H. Vincent, *Jérusalem de l'Ancien Testament*, I, pl. LXXXIII. Cf. *RB* (1925) XXXIV, p. 275 seq, and pl. xiii.

61.   Cf. Mark 16:3.

62.   Cf. Mark. 16:5; John 20:12.

63.   Luke 24:12; John 20:7. While the body was sometimes laid in a stone sarcophagus which was then placed in the tomb-chamber (the *topos* of Mark 16:6), it was generally wrapped in a shroud and laid on the bare rock of the tomb.

64.   John 20:5.

65.   F. de Zulueta, *Journal of Roman Studies* (1932), XXII, ii, p. 184 seq. He assigned it to the time of Augustus on palaeographical grounds.

66.   Cf. Acts 11:28, 18:2. The inscription was first published by the Abbé Cumont in *Revue historique* (1930), CLXIII, p. 241 seq., and dated epigraphically between 50 B.C. and A.D. 50 by scholars.

Cf. É. Cuq, *Revue d'histoire de Droit* (1930), IX, p. 383 seq.; F-M. Abel, *RB* (1930), XXXIX, p. 567 seq.; R. Tonneau, *RB* (1931), XL, p. 544 seq.; A. Momigliano, *L'opera dell' imperatore Claudio* (1931), p. 73 n 1.; G. Corradi, *Il Mondo classico* (1931), I, p. 56 seq.; W. F. Albright, *BASOR* (1959), No. 156, p. 41 f.

67. Cf. Matt. 28:13.

CHAPTER IV

1. The dictum of F. C. Bauer, quoted by A. T. Robertson, *Luke the Historian in the Light of Research* (1920), p. 1.

2. W. M. Ramsay, *Pauline and Other Studies* (1906), p. 199.

3. *PTRC*, p. 4.

4. R. Morgenthaler, *Die Lukanische Geschichtsschreibung als Zeugnis* (1940), II, p. 25.

5. E. Haenchen, *Die Apostelgeschichte* (Kritisch-Exegetischer Kommentar über das Neue Testament, III), 1959, pp. 90, 99.

6. B. Gärtner, *The Areopagus Speech and Natural Revelation* (1955), pp. 26 ff., 33 ff.

7. A. Ehrhardt, *Studia Theologica* (1958), XII, p. 45 seq. Cf. M. Dibelius, *Studies in the Acts of the Apostles* (1956), p. 125.; C. S. C. Williams, *ET* (1962), LXXIII, p. 133 seq.

8. F. F. Bruce, *The Acts of the Apostles* (1951), p. 15.

9. Luke 3:1 f.

10. E.g., *History of the Peloponnesian War*, II, 2.

11. E.g., Acts 13:7; 16:19 f., 35; 17:6, 19; 18:12; 19:31, 35, 38; 28:7, 16.

12. Acts 9:1 seq.; 22:3 seq.; 26:2 seq.

13. Acts 11:26.

14. *WJ*, III, 2, 4.

15. G. W. Elderkin (Ed.), *Antioch on-the-Orontes, I: The Excavation of 1932* (1934); R. Stillwell (Ed.), *ibid. II: The Excavations 1937–1939* (1941).

16. Suet. *Claud*. XVIII, 2.

17. Dio Cass. LX, 11; Tacit. *Annals*, XII, 43.

18. *AJ*, III, 15, 3; XX, 2, 5; XX, 5, 2.

19. Gal. 2:1 seq.

20. *BA* (1948), XI, No. 4, p. 82. The first phrase is reminiscent of the LXX of 1 Kgs. 16:4.

21. *BA* (1941), IV, No. 4. pl. 1.

22. *AJA* (1916), XX, p. 426 seq.

23. For a review of the history and literature of the subject cf. *BA* (1941), IV, No. 4, p. 49 seq.; *ibid.* (1942), V, No. 1, p. 1 seq.; *id.* (1948), XI, No. 4, p. 86 f.

24. E.g., C. R. Morey, *Art Studies* (1925), III, p. 73 seq.

25. Acts 13:4.

26. Cf. *ARE*, II, Sect. 493, 511, where it is spoken of as "Isy". During the Biblical period copper was mined extensively in the mountains of Cyprus, and it was from this that the island received its name.

27. *PTRC*, p. 74. Cf. Acts 13:7.

28. *WBA*, p. 249.

29. *PTRC*, p. 104.

30. *BRD*, pp. 150 ff.

31. D. M. Robinson, *AJA* (1924), XXVIII, p. 435 seq.

32. Xenophon (*Anabasis*, I, 2, 19) regarded it as the last city of Phrygia; Strabo (*Geography* 12, 6, 1) assigned it to the district of Lycaonia; also Pliny (*Hist. Nat.* V, 25).

33. Acts 14:6. This was one of the facts which early convinced Ramsay of the accuracy of St. Luke as an author. Cf. *BRD*, pp. 35 seq., 53 seq. The esteem in which Ramsay's work is still held by archaeologists is apparent from the comment by G. E. Wright, "Sir William Ramsay has probably done more in recovering the archaeological, historical and cultural background of the Pauline journeys in Asia Minor than any other modern scholar." *WBA*, p. 251 n 8.

34. Acts 14:6, 11.

35. LAP, pl. 115. Cf. W. M. Ramsay, *A Historical Commentary on St. Paul's Epistle to the Galatians* (1900), p. 224.

36. Probably Zeus.

37. These names in the A.V. are the Latin forms of the Greek names. Cf. *ET* (1925), XXXVII, p. 528.; *Discovery* (1926), VII, p. 262.

38. Cf. *The Expositor* (1910), VII, 10, p. 1 seq.; *Classical Review* (1910), XXIV, pp. 76 ff.; *ibid.* (1924), XXXVIII, p. 29 n 1.

39. Acts 15:1 seq.

40. W. M. Ramsay, *The Cities of St. Paul* (1907), pp. 262 f., 343, 401.

41. Cf. P. W. Schmiedel in *Encyclopaedia Biblica* (1899), col. 1592 seq.; J. Moffatt, *An Introduction to the Literature of the New Testament* (1918), p. 90 seq.

42. Acts 15:36 seq.

43. Acts 16:1 seq.

44. *PTRC*, p. 179.

45. Acts 16:2.

46. Acts 16:6.

47. Cf. K. and S. Lake, *An Introduction to the New Testament* (1938), pp. 85 ff., 129 f.; D. B. Knox, *Evangelical Quarterly* (1941), XIII, pp. 262 ff. For a

more recent study of early Christianity in Asia Minor *vide* S. E. Johnson, *JBL* (1958), LXXVII, p. 1 seq.

48. Acts 16:12 seq.

49. *Bulletin de correspondence hellénique* (1920), XLIV, p. 406 f.; *ibid.* (1921), XLV p. 543 seq.; *id.* (1922), XLVI, p. 527 seq.; *id.* (1923), XLVII, p. 534 seq.; *id.* (1924), XLVIII, p. 501.; *id.* (1925), XLIX, p. 462.; *id.* (1928), LII, p. 492 f.; *id.* (1930), LIV, p. 502 seq.; *id.* (1931), LV, p. 499 seq.; *id.* (1933), LVII, p. 279 seq.; *id.* (1934), LVIII, p. 257 seq.; *id.* (1935), LIX, p. 285 seq.; *id.* (1936), LX, pp. 478 ff.; *id.* (1937), LXI, p. 463 seq.; *id.* (1938), LXII, p. 1 seq.

50. *MM*, p. 398.

51. F. F. Bruce, *The Acts of the Apostles*, p. 313.

52. *PTRC*, p. 206 f.

53. Acts 16:13. The A.V., "we went out of the city by a river side" is incorrect, and should read, "we went forth beyond the gate beside a river."

54. Cf. W. A. MacDonald, *BA* (1940), III, No. 2, p. 18 seq.; *ibid. BA* (1941), IV, No. 1, p. 1 seq.

55. The *Stratēgoi* of Acts 16:20.

56. *De Leg. Agr.* II, 93.

57. Acts 17:6, 8.

58. Cf. E. D. Burton, *The American Journal of Theology* (1898), II, p. 598 seq.; *WBA*, p. 257.

59. Acts 18:5.

60. Since 1931 the American School of Classical Studies at Athens has spent a great deal of time and money in restoring the *agora*. Cf. T. L. Shear, *Hesperia* (1933), II, pp. 96 seq., 451 seq.; *ibid.* (1935), IV, pp. 311 seq., 340 seq.; *id.* (1936), V, p. 1 seq.; *id.* (1937), VI, p. 333 seq.; *id.* (1938), VII, p. 311 seq.; *id.* (1939), VIII, p. 201 seq.;

id. (1940), IX, p. 261 seq.; *id.* (1941), X, p. 1 seq. For a plan of the principal archaeological monuments of ancient Athens cf. *WBA*, pl. 204.

61. Acts 17:17. Cf. O. Broneer, *BA* (1958), XXI, No. 1, p. 17.

62. Acts 17:19 seq.

63. *WBA*, pl. 205.

64. "Areopagus" in Acts 17:19, 22 may refer either to the court itself or to the hill where it normally met. Most probably the speech was actually delivered from the hill itself.

65. Acts 17:23.

66. Acts 17:22.

67. E.g., Philostratus, *Vita Apoll. Tyan.* VI, 3, 5. "It is a proof of wisdom to speak well of all the gods, particularly at Athens, where altars are even erected in honour of unknown gods." Cf. Pausanias, I, 1, 4.; V, 14, 8.

68. *LAP*, pl. 119.

69. A. Deissmann, *Paul, A Study in Social and Religious History* (1926), pp. 288 ff.

70. For reports prior to the Second World War *vide AJA* (1930), XXXIV, p. 403 seq.; *ibid.* (1933), XXXVII, p. 554 seq.; *id.* (1935), XXXIX, p. 53 seq.; *id.* (1936) XL, pp. 21 seq., 466 seq.; *id.* (1937), XLI, p. 539 seq.; *id.* (1938), XLII, p. 362 seq.; *id.* (1939), XLIII, pp. 255 seq., 592 seq.

71. *BA* (1962), XXV, No. 1, p. 4 f.

72. For a plan of the central area of ancient Corinth *vide WBA*, pl. 207.

73. Acts 18:2 f.

74. Only the seven letters GOGEEBR could be deciphered readily. The inscription was first published by B. Powell, *AJA* (1903), VII, p. 60 f.

75. *I.e.*, [SUNA]GOGE EBR[AION].

76. A. Deissmann, *Licht vom Osten, das Neue Testament und die neuentdekten Texte der hellenistisch-römischen Welt* (1923), p. 12 n 8.

77. Cf. W. A. MacDonald, *BA* (1942), V. No. 3, p. 41.

78. *WBA*, p. 261. Cf. W. F. Albright, *Recent Discoveries in Bible Lands*, p. 119.

79. 1 Cor. 10:25. Cf. H. J. Cadbury, *JBL* (1934), LIII, p. 134 seq.

80. The *bēma* of Acts 18:12. Cf. *BA* (1951), XIV, No. 4 p. 91 f.

81. A. Deissmann, *Paul, A Study in Social and Religious History*, pp. 261 ff, 272 n.

82. *PTRC*, p. 258.

83. *PTRC*, p. 260.

84. *WBA*, pl. 209. It read, ERASTVS PRO: AED: S: P: STRAVIT. ("Erastus, procurator and aedile laid this pavement at his own expense."). Cf. F. F. Bruce, *Are the New Testament Documents Reliable?*, p. 92.

85. Acts 19:22.

86. Rom. 16:23. Cf. 2 Tim. 4:20. H. J. Cadbury, *JBL* (1931), L, p. 48 seq., expressed doubts about the identification.

87. 1 Cor. 9:7.

88. 1 Cor. 8:10.

89. 1 Cor. 9:24 seq. Cf. *BA* (1962), XXV, No. 1, p. 2 seq.

90. *BA* (1951), XIV, No. 4, p. 96.

91. Acts 18:18.

CHAPTER V

1. B. H. Streeter, *JTS* (1933), XXXIV, p. 237, interpreted the ambiguity of the Greek text of Acts 18:22 in terms of Caesarea rather than

Jerusalem. However, the verb *katabainō* would not be used for a journey from a seaport (Caesarea) to an inland town (Antioch).

2. Acts 19:1 seq.

3. This may be the "throne of Satan" of Rev. 2:13.

4. Strabo, *Geography*, XIV, 1, 24.

5. Cf. Acts 19:24.

6. J. T. Wood, *Modern Discoveries on the Site of Ancient Ephesus* (1890), p. 37 seq.

7. D. G. Hogarth, *Excavations at Ephesus, The Archaic Artemisia* (1908); Cf. *Forschungen in Ephesos, veröffentlicht vom Österreichischen archaeologischen Institute* (1906–37), 4 vols.

8. *WBA*, pl. 200.

9. Cf. Acts 19:28, 34. W. M. Ramsay, *The Church in the Roman Empire before A.D. 170* (1912), p. 135 seq.; *BA* (1945), VIII, No. 3, p. 67 seq.

10. Acts 19:29.

11. *WBA*, pl. 201.

12. Traditionally Artemis fell down from heaven, and was probably of meteoric origin like the Palladium of Troy and other objects of religious veneration in antiquity.

13. The Greek *neokoros* or "temple sweeper" was used as a title of honour for individuals [*BA* (1945), VIII, No. 4, p. 80], and sometimes for an entire group (cf. *WJ*, V, 9, 4.). For an inscription proclaiming Ephesus as "Warden of the Temple of Artemis" *vide Corpus Inscriptionum Graecarum*, No. 2972.

14. Acts 19:13.

15. A. Deissmann, *Bible Studies* (1909), p. 322 seq.; *ibid. Light From the Ancient East*, p. 254 seq.

16. Acts 19:18.

17. Acts 19:31.

18. Acts 20:17 ff.

19. Rom. 15:23 f.

20. Acts 21:28.

21. *WJ*, V, 5, 2; VI, 2, 4; *AJ*, XV, 11, 5.

22. *Palestine Exploration Fund Quarterly* (1871), p. 132.; Cf. *Quarterly of the Department of Antiquities in Palestine* (1938), VI, p. 1 seq.; W. F. Albright, *Recent Discoveries in Bible Lands*, p. 112; A. Parrot, *Le Musée du Louvre et la Bible*, p. 142 f.

23. Acts 27:12. The Greek has "down the south-west wind and down the north-west wind." The R.V. reads, "looking north-east and south-east"; the R.S.V. margin reads, "looking southwest and northwest" and N.E.B. has "exposed south-west and north-west."

24. J. Smith, *The Voyage and Shipwreck of St. Paul* (1866), pp. 87 seq., 252 seq.

25. *PTRC*, p. 325 f.

26. *JTS* (1958), IX, pp. 308 ff.

27. The *prōtos* of Acts 28:7.

28. *Inscriptiones Graecae* (1873–), XIV, 60.

29. *Corpus Inscriptionum Latinarum*, X, No. 7495.

30. Acts 28:13.

31. For a survey of early Christian evidences at Pompeii *vide* F. V. Filson, *BA* (1939), II, No. 2, p. 13 seq.

32. Acts 28:15.

33. Roman law prohibited burials within the city limits.

34. Cf. H. Lietzmann, *Petrus und Paulus in Rom* (1927), p. 246 f.

35. Cf. Eusebius, *Hist. Eccl.*, II, 25, 7.

36. Cf. R. T. O'Callaghan, *BA* (1949), XII, No. 1, p. 2 seq.; *ibid. BA* (1953), XVI, No. 4, p. 70 seq.;

O. Cullmann, *Peter: Disciple, Apostle, Martyr* (1953), p. 132 seq.; R. K. Harrison, *The Churchman* (1955), LXIX, No. 2, p. 94 seq.

37. Hom. *Od.*, XIV, 152.

38. Isoc. VII, 10; Aristoph. *Equit.* 656.

39. Gal. 1:11 *et al.*; *MM*, p. 259.

40. Polyb. I, 51, 6; XVI, 6, 2.

41. Eubul. *Nausik.* I, 68.

42. Plat. *Sympos.* 176b

43. Plutar. *Galb.* 21.

44. Aristopho, XIV, 5.

45. *MM*, p. 102.

46. 1 Pet. 5:5 *et al.*

47. Arrian, *Epict. Disser.* III, 24.

48. *WJ*, IV, 9, 2.

49. Oxyr. Pap. I, 79.

50. Cf. *MM*, p. 625.

51. 2 Cor. 1:22; 5:5; Eph. 1:14.

52. Grenf. Pap. II, 67, 17 ff.; Milligan, *Selections From the Greek Papyri*, p. 109.

53. *MM*, p. 79. In modern Greek the word means an "engagement ring".

54. *MM*, p. 618.

55. Oxyr. Pap. VI, 932.

56. Rom. 15:28.

57. *LSCA*, p. 191.

58. Rev. 2:2 seq.

59. *LSCA*, p. 266 f. Cf. F. Stark, *Ionia, A Quest* (1954), p. 9.

60. Rev. 2:10.

61. *NAD*, p. 563 f.

62. In 1959, after being brought back from Russia.

63. Rev. 2:13.

64. Cf. E. M. Blaiklock, *The Christian in Pagan Society* (1951), p. 7 seq.

65. *LSCA*, p. 325.

66. Rev. 2:18.

67. *NAD*, p. 565 seq.; G. M. A. Hanfman, *BASOR* (1959), No. 154, p. 5 seq.

68. Rev. 3:3.

69. Rev. 3:8.

70. Rev. 3:14 seq. Cf. *LSCA*, p. 416 seq.

71. Rev. 3:15.

72. *ET* (1958), LXIX, pp. 176 ff. In antiquity luke-warm water was frequently used as an emetic. Cf. Rev. 3:16.

73. Rev. 13:18.

74. *WMTS*, p. 270.

75. The uncial C (fifth century A.D.) and two cursive manuscripts. Cf. *Patrologia Latina*, XXXV, Col. 2437. For the interpretation of the numbers cf. H. B. Swete, *The Apocalypse of St. John* (1909), p. 174 f.; R. H. Charles, *The Revelation of St. John* (International Critical Commentary, 1920), I, p. 364 seq.

76. For a study of the Beast of the Book of Revelation in the light of ancient Near Eastern archaeological discoveries cf. H. Wallace, *BA* (1948), XI, No. 3, p. 61 seq.

77. Rev. 17:9.

78. *WMTS*, p. 270.

CHAPTER VI

1. For a recent introduction to the first decade of work on the Qumran scrolls cf. R. K. Harrison, *The Dead Sea Scrolls* (Teach Yourself Series), 1961.

2. G. E. Wright, *BA* (1948) XI, No. 2, pp. 21 ff. Cf. *BA* (1948), XI, No. 3, p. 46 seq.

3. J. van der Ploeg, *The Excavations at Qumran* (1958), p. 189.

4. A Dupont-Sommer, *Aperçus préliminaires sur les manuscrits de la Mer Morte* (1950), p. 121 f.

5. A. Dupont-Sommer, *The Jewish Sect of Qumran and the Essenes* (1954), p. 160 seq.

6. January 23rd, 1956. Cf. his comments in *The Radio Times*, January 13th, 1956, p. 9.

7. Allegro's observations were based partly on a reference in the fragmentary commentary on Nahum (cf. JBL, 1956, LXXV, p. 91 seq.), recovered from the fourth Qumran cave. Taking a reference to hanging men up alive as an act of barbarity perpetrated by Alexander *c.* 88 B.C., (cf. *AJ*, XIII, 14, 1 f.; *WJ* I, 4, 6.), he concluded that the Righteous Teacher was crucified at this time also. Cf. J. M. Allegro, *The Dead Sea Scrolls* (1956), p. 95 seq.; *JBL* (1956) LXXV, p. 89 seq.

8. *The Times*, March 16th, 1956.

9. Edmund Wilson, *The Scrolls From the Dead Sea* (1955).

10. E. Wilson, *The Scrolls From the Dead Sea*, p. 108.

11. E. L. Sukenik published portions from the smaller Isaiah manuscript (1QISb), the War Scroll (1QM), and the Thanksgiving Hymns (1QH). in *Megilloth Genuzoth* (Vol. I, 1948; Vol. II, 1950), while the St. Mark's Monastery scrolls were published by M. Burrows (Ed.), *The Dead Sea Scrolls from St. Mark's Monastery: Vol. I, The Isaiah Manuscript and the Habakkuk Commentary* (1950); *Vol. II, Fasc. 2, Plates and Transcription of the Manual of Discipline* (1951). Other scrolls and fragments have been published in photostatic or transcribed form with equal promptness, and are

accessible to all those who are interested in their contents. However, only a small portion of the total fragments recovered has been published to date.

12. A. Powell Davies, *The Meaning of the Dead Sea Scrolls* (1956).

13. Such objections as these have been answered decisively by a lay scholar, Professor F. F. Bruce, in his work *Second Thoughts on the Dead Sea Scrolls* (1961 ed.), p. 137 seq.

14. *SSNT*, p. 1 seq., where the issues raised by Wilson are discussed thoroughly.

15. 1QS, V:1 ff.

16. 1QS, V:13 ff.

17. Cf. 1QS, V:3 ff.

18. 1QpHab, VII:3 ff.

19. Their rule of life required them to await the arrival of a prophet and two Messianic figures who were styled "the anointed ones of Aaron and Israel." Cf. 1QS, IX:11; CDC, XII: 23 seq., XIV: 19 XIX: 10 f., XX: 1; J. T. Milik, *RB* (1953), LX, p. 291. In the *Testament of the Twelve Patriarchs* a Davidic and Levitical Messiah were expected to appear in the last days. Cf. K. G. Kuhn, *NTS* (1955), I, p. 168 seq.

20. Deut. 18:18 f.

21. Cf. J. M. Allegro, *The Dead Sea Scrolls*, pp. 138 ff.

22. A quotation from the Balaam oracles about a star rising from Jacob (Num. 24:15 ff.), and the blessing of the Levites by Moses (Deut. 33:8 seq.) constituted important elements of this florilegium, which concluded with a passage from an hitherto unknown pseudepigraphal work.

23. For a free translation *vide DSSET*, p. 307 seq. Cf. D. Barthélemy, *RB* (1952), LIX, pp. 203 ff.

24. Identified by Milik with the Messiah of Aaron, *RB* (1953), LX, p. 291.

25. It should be noted that the Righteous Teacher was never identified with either of these two personages. Cf. J. van der Ploeg, *Bibliotheca Orientalis* (1951), VIII, p. 13. For the suggestion that the title "Righteous Teacher" denotes a continuing office rather than a particular individual *vide DSSET*, p. 26. For an examination of the concepts of the two Messiahs cf. K. G. Kuhn, *SSNT*, p. 54 seq.

26. The procedure adopted at this meal has much in common with what Josephus recorded about the Essene sacramental meal. Cf. *WJ*, II, 8, 5.

27. J. Allegro, *The Dead Sea Scrolls*, p. 90, questioned the use of the cisterns for baptismal rites, but since the Qumran texts mention ritual washings on several occasions (1QS, III:4 f., 9; V:13 f. Cf. CDC, XII:1 f.), where regulations were prescribed for ritual purification (cf. *AJ*, XVIII, 1, 5; *WJ*, II, 7, 5.), it seems probable that they were in fact employed frequently for this purpose.

28. A large crack running down the centre of the steps and continuing into an adjacent area may have been caused by an earth tremor in 31 B.C., when the site was apparently unoccupied for a time. Cf. *AJ*, XV, 5, 2; *WJ*, I, 19, 3.

29. 1QS, V:13 f.

30. 1QS, III:4 seq.

31. The Qumran community council comprised three priests (cf. Gal. 2:9) and twelve laymen. 1QS, VIII:1. Cf. 1QS, V:19.

32. The equivalent of *paqidh* in 1QS, VI:14.

33. Heb. 12:24. Cf. Heb. 7:22 seq.

34. Cf. W. H. Brownlee, *United Presbyterian* (1953), November 30, December 7, 14, 21, 28.

35. Mark 14:24; Luke 22:20; 1 Cor. 11:25. The Markan expression "took bread, and blessed, and brake it "is the typical *paterfamilias* Jewish usage, presupposing Semitic rather than Hellenistic origins.

36. Cf. K. G. Kuhn, *SSNT*, pp. 90 ff. For an attempt to equate the Passover with the Lord's Supper *vide* A. J. B. Higgins, *The Lord's Supper in the New Testament* (1952), p. 13 seq.

37. A list of vices said to result from the activity of the spirit of perversity in the human personality is contained in 1QS, IV:1 seq.

38. *SSNT*, p. 10 f.

39. *CALQ*, p. 90.

40. The identification of the Qumran group with the Essenes, following Milik, is so frequently assumed as a matter of course by many scholars, *e.g.*, D. Howlett, *The Essenes and Christianity* (1959). For a protest against this view *vide* C. Rabin, *Qumran Studies* (1957), pp. 59 f., 69 f., who argues that they were basically Pharisaic (a position criticized by J. M. Baumgarten, *JBL* (1958), LXXVII, p. 249 seq.); C. Roth, *The Historical Background of the Dead Sea Scrolls* (1958), p. 12 *passim*, who equated them with the Zealots of the first century A.D.; J. L. Teicher, *JJS* (1951), II, pp. 67 seq., 115 seq., who identified them with the first century A.D. Ebionites; R. Marcus, *JBL* (1954), LXXIII, p. 161, who regarded them as Gnosti-cizing Pharisees. For a study of Roth's theory cf. R. de Vaux, *RB* (1959), LXVI, p. 102.; H. H. Rowley, *VT* (1959), IX, p. 379 seq. In the opinion of the present writer the Qumran sectaries can only be identified with the Essene groups in a very general way, if at all. Cf. R. K. Harrison, *The Dead Sea Scrolls*, p. 95 seq.

41. The concept of ceremonial purification of objects and persons by means of water reaches back to the

Mosaic era. Cf. Exod. 19:10 seq.; Lev. 8:6;
Mark 7:3 f.; Heb. 9:10. According to Rabbinical
teachings baptism, next to circumcision and
sacrifice, was an absolute and necessary condition
which a proselyte to Judaism was required to
fulfil. Cf. *Yer. Kid.* iii, 14, 64d.; '*Ab Zarah* 57a;
Shab. 135a; *Yeb.* 46b. 47b; *Ker.* 9a; *Yoma* viii, 9.

42. 1QS, III:4 seq.; V:13 f.

43. The connection between the *Zadokite Fragment*
     (CDC), which issued from the Damascene
     Covenanters, and the Qumran material was
     pointed out, among others, by E. L. Sukenik,
     Megilloth Genuzoth I, pp. 21 ff.; S. Zeitlin, *JQR*
     (1948–49), XXXIX, p. 274.; I. L. Seeligmann,
     Bibliotheca Orientalis (1949), VI, p. 5; B. Reicke,
     Studia Theologica (1949–50), II, pp. 45 ff.; M.
     Burrows, *Oudtestamentische Studiën* (1950), VIII,
     pp. 167, 180 ff.; B. J. Roberts, *BJRL* (1951–52),
     XXXIV, pp. 366 ff.; H. H. Rowley, *The Zadokite
     Fragments and the Dead Sea Scrolls* (1952), p. 31 seq.
     G. R. Driver, *The Hebrew Scrolls from the Neigh-
     bourhood of Jericho and the Dead Sea* (1951), p. 22,
     questioned the possibility of absolute identifica-
     tion of the two groups, and asserted that undoubt-
     ed proof will probably never be forthcoming.

44. CDC, XII:1 ff.

45. Ezek. 36:25 ff.

46. Cf. 1QS, III:6 seq.; IV:20 ff. As M. Black, *The
     Scrolls and Christian Origins* (1961), p. 98 n 1, has
     pointed out, the statement of Kuhn (*SSNT*, p. 77)
     that the Qumran rite was a baptism for sins is
     incorrect. It may, however, have been popularly
     assumed that cleansing from sin would be one
     result of participation in the rites, though this is
     nowhere explicitly taught in the Qumran liter-
     ature.

47. 1QS, IV:21 f.

48. Isa. 52:15. Cf. John 1:33.

49. Cf. 1QS, IX:11; CDC, II:9.

50. Matt. 3:7 seq.; Luke 3:3 seq.

51. Matt. 3:1.

52. Matt. 4:1.

53. John 11:54.

54. E. Wilson, *The Scrolls From the Dead Sea*, p. 129.

55. G. L. Harding, *The Illustrated London News*, September 3rd, 1955, p. 379. According to U. C. Ewing, *The Essene Christ* (1961), pp. 50 seq., 78 seq., Jesus was an Essene, a vegetarian, and the incarnation of the Righteous Teacher.

56. Luke 1:5 seq.

57. Luke 1:80.

58. The food of the Baptist is typical of the life of the desert nomad, who regularly included small insects such as grasshoppers or locusts in his diet. The "locusts" are thus most probably insect species, and not the "carob pods" of the prodigal son (Luke 15:16), otherwise they would doubtless have been referred to as "pods". Cf. W. H. Brownlee, *SSNT*, p. 33.

59. Matt. 3:7 seq.; Luke 3:3.

60. Matt. 3:3. John the Baptist was identified with the Righteous Teacher by R. Eisler, *Modern Churchman* (1949), XXXIX, p. 284 seq.

61. E.g., W. H. Brownlee, *BA* (1950), XIII, No. 3, p. 69 seq.; *ibid. Interpretation* (1955), IX, p. 71 seq.; B. Reicke, *Religion och Bibel* (1952), XI, p. 5 seq.; A. Metzinger, *Biblica* (1955), XXXVI, p. 457 seq.; A. S. Geyser, *NT* (1956), I, p. 70 seq.; E. Stauffer, *Theologische Literaturzeitung* (1956), LXXXI, col. 143 f.

62. Cf. D. Barthélemy and J. T. Milik, *Discoveries in*

the *Judean Desert I*, Qumran, Cave I (1955),
p. 108 seq.

63. Cf. *WJ*, II, 8, 2.

64. Cf. 1QS, VI:3; CDC, XV:5.

65. 1QS, X:20 f.; CDC, II:3. IX:41.

66. CDC, IX:15.

67. 1QS, III:6 seq.; V:13 f.

68. CDC, IX:10, 29; XV:4; XVIII:8.

69. John 1:23. Cf. Matt. 3:3; Mark 1:3.

70. Mark 1:8; John 1:33; Acts 1:5, 11:16.

71. Matt. 3:11 f.; Luke 3:16. Cf. *SSNT*, p. 42.

72. Cf. 1QS, VIII:13 f.

73. CF. J. A. T. Robinson, *Harvard Theological Review* (1957), I, No. 3, p. 177.

74. Mark 2:18; Luke 5:33, 11:1.

75. *CALQ*, p. 204 n 9. The group of disciples mentioned in Acts 19:1 seq. is an isolated occurrence of this sort.

76. Isa. 40:3.

77. John 1:26, 31, 33.

78. Matt. 11:19; Luke 7:34.

79. Matt. 9:14; Mark 2:18; Luke 5:33.

80. F. F. Bruce, *Second Thoughts on the Dead Sea Scrolls*, p. 144.

81. For a study of the relationship between Matt. 5–7 and the Qumran texts *vide* K. Schubert, *Theologische Quartalschrift* (1955), CXXXV, p. 320 seq., and translated in *SSNT*, p. 118 seq.

82. Cf. H. Strack and P. Billerbeck, *Kommentar zum Neuen Testament aus Talmud und Midrasch* (1922–28), 4 Vols.; C. G. Montefiore, *Commentary on the Synoptic Gospels* (1927); *ibid. Rabbinic Literature and*

  Gospel Teachings (1930); D. Daube, *The New Testament and Rabbinic Judaism* (1956), p. 55 seq.

83. Matt. 5:17.

84. 1QS, III:6 f.

85. John 8:12. Cf. 1QS, III:20, "All the sons of justice tread in the ways of light."

86. CDC, IX:21.

87. 1QS, X:19.

88. Matt. 6:24.

89. Matt. 12:9 seq.; Mark 3:1 seq.; Luke 6:6 seq.

90. CDC, XIII:23 f. Essene sabbath rules were generally much stricter than those of the Pharisees. For a contrast of the teaching of Christ with the tenets of the Qumran sectaries cf. H. H. Rowley, *BJRL* (1961), XLIV, p. 119.

91. In the Ethel M. Wood lectures delivered before the University of London on March 7th, 1961, J. Jeremias, *The Sermon on the Mount* (1961) took no cognisance of any relationship between Matthew 5 and the Qumran literature.

92. Matt. 5:3. Cf. Luke 6:20.

93. So H. L. Strack and P. Billerbeck, *Kommentar zum Neuen Testament aus Talmud und Midrasch*, I, p. 190.

94. IQH, II:32. Cf. 1QpHab, XII:3, 6, 10 and K. Elliger, *Studien zum Habakuk-Kommentar vom Toten Meer* (1953), pp. 221 ff.

95. Thus it is incorrect to suggest, as Schubert has done (*SSNT*, p. 122), that the "real sense of the passage" is in the meaning "poor in will, poor in inward agreement, voluntarily poor", for while the sect renounced monetary values, their prime emphasis was upon spiritual fidelity to the New Covenant.

96. Matt. 5:22.

97. 1QS, VI:1. Cf. 1QS, V:25 seq.

98.   Matt. 18:15 ff.

99.   Matt. 5:28. Cf. Exod. 20:14.

100. 1QS, I:6.

101. 1QS, IV:10.

102. 1QpHab, V:7.

103. CDC, VII:2 f.

104. Matt. 19:3 seq.

105. CDC, VII:3.

106. Matt. 5:33 seq.

107. *WJ*, II, 8, 6.; Cf. *AJ*, XV, 10, 4.

108. CDC, XIX:1.

109. Matt. 5:38 f.

110. 1QS, X:17 f. For a study of the use made by the covenanters of Old Testament quotations, cf. J. A. Fitzmyer, *NTS* (1961), VII, p. 297.

111. Cf. 1QS, II:8; IV:2 seq; 1QpHab, V:4.

112. Isa. 52:14 *et al*. Cf. 1QS, IV:20.; W. H. Brownlee, *BASOR* (1953), No. 132, pp. 10 ff.

113. 1QS, VIII:4 seq.; cf. 1QS, IV:22.

114. J. van der Ploeg, *The Excavations at Qumran*, p. 207.

115. An extensive literature on the topic includes the following: K. G. Kuhn, *Zeitschrift für Theologie und Kirche* (1950), XLVII, p. 209 f.; W. Grossouw, *Studia Catholica* (1951), XXVI, p. 295 seq.; L. Mowry, *BA* (1954), XVII, No. 4, p. 78 seq.; F. M. Braun, *RB* (1955), LXII, p. 5 seq.; S. Mowinckel, *JBL* (1956), LXXV, p. 276; W. F. Albright in W. D. Davies and D. Daube (Ed.), *The Background of the New Testament and Its Eschatology* (1956), p. 163 seq.

116. Cf. John 1:35; W. H. Brownlee, *BA* (1950), XIII, No. 3, p. 72; J. A. T. Robinson, *Harvard Theological Review* (1957), I, No. 3, p. 190.

117. John 1:3. No precise equivalent of the Johannine sense can as yet be documented in the scrolls.

118. 1QS, XI:11. Cf. 1QS, III:15 ff.

119. John 12:36. Cf. 1QS, I:9; 1QM *passim*.

120. John 3:15 f. *et passim*. Cf. 1QS, II:2 f.; IV:7 *et al.*

121. John 14:17; 15:26; 16:13; 1 John 4:2. Cf. 1QS, III:13—IV:26.

122. John 8:12; 11:10; 12:35; 1 John 1:6 f.; 2:11. Cf. 1QS, III:20 f.

123. John 8:12. Cf. 1QS, III:15.

124. John 6:28; 9:3. Cf. 1QS, IV:4.

125. E.g., 1 John 2:15; 3:13. Cf. R. E. Brown, *Catholic Biblical Quarterly* (1955), XVII, p. 561 seq.

126. 1QS, I:9 f.

127. John 17:11, 21, 23.

128. For John 17:23 cf. 1QS, V:2; for John 11:52 cf. 1QS, V:7.

129. The term "community" (*hyḥd*) means literally "togetherness" or "unity" with a primary eschatological, rather than a merely social, emphasis.

130. 1 John 3:7 seq.

131. 1 John 4:1 seq.

132. Cf. 1QS, III:17 seq., IV:1 seq.; K. G. Kuhn, *Zeitschrift für Theologie und Kirche* (1950), XLVII, p. 192 seq.; *ibid.* (1952), XLIX, p. 245 seq. For the Qumran doctrine of the Spirit *vide* W. D. Davies in *SSNT*, p. 157 seq.

133. O. J. Baab, *The Theology of the Old Testament* (1949) p. 234.

134. W. F. Albright in *The Background of the New Testament and Its Eschatology*, p. 170, has listed four ways in which Johannine theology differed from Essenism.

135.   Kirsopp Lake, *An Introduction to the New Testament*,
       p. 53.

136.   J. A. Montgomery, *The Origin of the Gospel Accord-
       ing to St. John* (1923), p. 30. Cf. A. M. Hunter,
       ET (1960), LXXI, pp. 164, 219, who urged a
       Palestinian origin for the Fourth Gospel and
       dated it *c*. 80 A.D., or even as early as 70 A.D.
       Cf. C. L. Mitton, *ET* (1960), LXXI, p. 337;
       W. F. Albright, *Christianity Today* (1963), VII,
       No. 8, p. 359.

137.   Cf. S. E. Johnson, *Zeitschrift für die alttestamentliche
       Wissenschaft* (1954), LXVI, p. 106 seq.; F. M.
       Cross, *The Christian Century*, August 24th, 1955,
       p. 968 seq.; J. Daniélou, *Revue d'histoire et de
       philosophie religieuses* (1955), XXXV, p. 104 seq.;
       B. Reicke, *SSNT*, p. 143 seq.

138.   Cf. E. Schweizer, *Das Leben des Herrn in der
       Gemeinde und ihren Diensten* (1946), pp. 23 *passim*.

139.   Cf. W. Michaelis, *Das Aeltestenamt der christlichen
       Gemeinde im Lichte der Heiligen Schrift* (1953), p. 26
       passim.

140.   K. E. Kirk (Ed.), *The Apostolic Ministry* (1946),
       pp. vi, 10, 311. Not all the contributors are so
       emphatic about the form of the "Apostolic
       succession."

141.   Acts 20:17, 28.

142.   The concept that bishops are a higher form of
       ministry, indeed of the *esse* of the Church, specially
       endowed and blessed by God to dispense the gifts
       of the Holy Spirit, is not found in the New Testa-
       ment, and is a late accretion of tradition. In the
       New Testament all true believers, whether elders,
       deacons or laymen are alike members of the "holy
       nation," and exercise the "royal priesthood", the
       difference being merely one of function, not
       status.

143.   The equivalent of *paqidh* in 1QS, VI:14, and

probably the same as *epimelētēs*, used of the Essene
overseers by Jospehus. Cf. *CALQ*, p. 232 f.

144.   1QS, VIII:1. Cf. 1QS, VI:19.

145.   Cf. CDC, XIII:7 seq.; *CALQ*, p. 232.

146.   Cf. Isa. 53:6; 61:1; Ezek. 34:12. In Isa. 40:11
       God is described as a shepherd who nourishes
       His flock.

147.   John 10:14. The association of this concept with
       the Atonement is of great importance.

148.   1 Pet. 2:25.

149.   1 Cor. 4:1.

150.   Gal. 3:28; Col. 3:11 *et al.*

151.   1QS, II:24 f.

152.   1QS, I:11 f. Cf. 1QS, V:2. This was similar to
       Essene practices. Cf. *WJ*, II, 8, 3. Upon being
       formally admitted, the Qumran novice assigned
       his property for communal purposes. Cf. 1QS,
       VI:21 f.

153.   Acts 4:32.

154.   Acts 2:44 f.; 4:32 seq., 5:1.

155.   Cf. CDC, XIV:12 ff.

156.   E.g., Rom. 6:19; 7:5, 18, 25; 8:3 seq.; 2 Cor.
       1:17, *et al.* Cf. K. G. Kuhn, *SSNT*, p. 101 seq.

157.   E.g., 1QpHab, IV:29, IX:3; 1QS, III:6 ff.,
       XI:9; 1QM, IV:3. Cf. W. D. Davies, *SSNT*,
       p. 160 seq.

158.   Cf. 1QS, III:13—IV:26; W. D. Davies, *SSNT*,
       p. 171 seq.

159.   1 Cor. 2:12.

160.   Rom. 8:9; 1 John 4:2, *et al.*

161.   Cf. Rom. 1:29 ff., 13:13; Gal. 5:19 f.; Col. 3:5, 8.

162.   1QS, IV:1 seq.

163. 1QH, I:26 f., IV:30 f., 40, *et al.*

164. 1QS, XI:2 f., 13 ff.

165. 1QpHab, VIII:1 seq.

166. E.g., Rom. 3–5; Gal. 2:16—3:29; Eph. 2:8 *et al.*

167. Jas. 1:12.

168. Cf. 1QS, VIII:4; 1QH, II:35, VIII:26 seq., IX:6 seq., XI:19 seq.

169. Jas. 1:12.

170. 1QS, IV:7.

171. Jas. 4:5.

172. 1QS, IV:9 seq.

173. Cf. *DSSET*, p. 16 f.

174. Jude, vs. 9, 14 f.

175. E.g., A. S. Peake, *A Critical Introduction to the New Testament* (1910), p. 99.; F. B. Clogg, *An Introduction to the New Testament* (1937), p. 172.; R. Heard, *An Introduction to the New Testament* (1950), p. 219.; A. H. McNeile, *An Introduction to the Study of the New Testament* (1955 ed.), pp. 247 ff.

176. J. Jeremias (*ET*, 1958, LXIX, pp. 68 ff.) has assessed the significance of the scrolls for the New Testament in terms of illuminating the historical background of Jesus, and particularly as demonstrating how completely new the message of Jesus was.

177. Cf. F. M. Cross, *The New Republic*, April 9th, 1956, p. 18 f.

178. *CALQ*, p. 242 f.

179. In his presidential address to the Society of Biblical Literature and Exegesis in December, 1961.

Chapter VII

1. For a survey of the material *vide* T. Mina, *Vigiliae Christianae* (1948), II, p. 129 seq.; J. Doresse, *ibid.* (1948), II, p. 137 seq.; *id.* (1949), III, p. 129 seq.; J. Doresse, *La Nouvelle Clio* (1949), I, p. 59 seq.; H-Ch. Puech, *Coptic Studies in Honour of Walter Ewing Crum* (1950), p. 91 seq.; W. C. Till, *JEA* (1952), III, p. 14 seq.; V. R. Gold, *BA* (1952), XV, No. 4, p. 70 seq.; A. D. Nock, *JTS* (1958), VIII, p. 314 seq.; G. Quispel, *NTS* (1959), V, p. 273 seq.; R. McL. Wilson, *Studies in the Gospel of Thomas* (1960), p. 14 seq.

2. Unsubstantiated rumours have persisted to the effect that some of the scrolls were burned for fuel by the peasants.

3. These include the *Revelation of Adam to his Son Seth*, the *Second Treatise of the Great Seth*, the *Gospel of the Egyptians*, the *Three Steles of Seth*, and the *Hypostasis of the Archons*. It should be noted that Seth (Set) was also the name of an important Egyptian deity who was the adversary of Osiris in the religious and mythological texts of ancient Egypt. Cf. J. H. Breasted, *Development of Religion and Thought in Ancient Egypt* (1959), p. 25 *passim*.

4. These include such titles as the *Dialogue of the Saviour*, the *Revelation of James*, the *Apocryphon of John*, the *Wisdom of Jesus* and the *Gospel According to Thomas*.

5. A. Guillamont, H-Ch. Puech, G. Quispel, W. Till and Yassah 'Abd Al Masiḥ (Trans.), *The Gospel According to Thomas* (1959).

6. While some have again predicted that certain basic Christian teachings would need to be revised drastically in the light of this discovery, and others have called the document a "Fifth Gospel", such expectations are completely un-

justified by the facts of the case. Cf. B. Gärtner, *The Theology of the Gospel According to Thomas* (1961), p. 11.

7. The first edition of *GAT* contained one hundred and fourteen *logia*.

8. B. P. Grenfell and A. S. Hunt, *The Oxyrhynchus Papyri* (1898), Part I; *ibid.* (1904), Part IV. Cf. H. G. E. White, *The Sayings of Jesus From Oxyrhynchus* (1920).

9. The Greek text here includes one sentence which was omitted from the Coptic.

10. Ox. Pap. 654, lines 9–21; *GAT*, *logion* 3, p. 3.

11. Ox. Pap. 1, Lines 24–31; *GAT*, logion 77b, p. 43.

12. Cf. M. R. James, *The Apocryphal New Testament* (1924), p. 49 seq.

13. In Lucam Homiliae I, *Patrologiae Graecae* XIII, Col. 1803.

14. *Hist. Eccl.* III, 25, 6.

15. Hippolytus, *The Refutation of All Heresies*, V, 2. (Transl. in *The Ante-Nicene Fathers* (1951), V, p. 50.).

16. *GAT*, *logion* 4, p. 3.

17. Cyril of Jerusalem, *Catecheses* IV, 36., VI, 31.

18. These are *logia* 24, 38, 43 and 77.

19. For a comparison of related Coptic *logia* with the Synoptic Gospels cf. H. K. McArthur, *New Testament Sidelights* (Essays in Honour of Alexander Converse Purdy, 1960), p. 57 seq.

20. Thus it is unlikely that Christ would have spoken of "James the righteous" in *logion* 12.

21. The strange parable of children taking over a field which is not their property (*logion* 21a) appears to be part of a "Gnostic" dialogue between Mary and Christ.

22.   Acts 20:35.

23.   *GAT, logion* 25, p. 19.

24.   *GAT, logion* 82, p. 45. Cf. Origen, Homilies on Jeremiah, XX, 3, *Patrologiae Graecae*, XIII, Col. 277.

25.   John 8:46.

26.   *GAT, logion* 104, p. 53.

27.   Matt. 5:3 seq.

28.   *GAT, logion* 58, p. 33.

29.   The original Greek concept of *gnosis* or *rational knowledge* was modified by the Gnostics into a charismatic gift, the possession of which makes a man divine. Cf. R. Bultmann in R. Kittel (Ed.), *Theologisches Wörterbuch zum Neuen Testament* (1933) I, pp. 693 ff.

30.   Because of their belief in the essentially evil nature of matter, the Gnostics could never accept a real incarnation of Christ. Cf. R. McL. Wilson, *The Gnostic Problem* (1958), p. 104.

31.   Cf. E. Hatch, *The Influence of Greek Ideas and Usages upon the Christian Church* (1904), p. 190 seq.

32.   For the Gnostics salvation was obtained through a mystic *gnosis* imparted by the Redeemer, and not as a result of faith in the finished atonement of Calvary.

33.   *GAT, logion* 56, p. 31. Cf. *logion* 110, p. 55.

34.   *GAT, logion* 42, p. 25. Occasionally "world" has the force of "world of men." Cf. *logion* 24.

35.   *GAT, logion* 29, p. 21. Cf. *logion* 87, p. 47.

36.   This is in marked contrast to the New Testament, in which it is urged that what formerly was mysterious is now made manifest. Cf. Matt. 10:26; Mark 4:22; Luke 8:17, 12:2; Col. 1:26 f.

37.   *GAT, logion* 3b, p. 3.

38. *GAT*, *logion* 67, p. 39.

39. *GAT*, *logion* 7, p. 5.

40. *GAT*, *logion* 114b, p. 57.

41. *GAT*, *logion* 14, p. 11.

42. Bultmann has interpreted Gnosticism in terms of a world-wide syncretistic movement drawing upon the resources of many pre-Christian religions, and has seen such New Testament terms as "god of this world" (2 Cor. 4:4), "ruler of this world" (John 12:31), "principalities", "powers", and "rulers of this present darkness" (Eph. 6:12) as survivals of Gnostic religious terminology. Cf. R. Bultmann, *Theologie des Neuen Testaments* (1948), p. 255 f.

43. Bultmann holds that the New Testament picture of Christ is nothing more than an adaptation of a pre-Christian Iranian Gnostic redemptive figure. This mythical "redeemed Redeemer" corresponds to the first Man, created in the image of the highest Deity, and is an intermediary between man and the unknown Creator. Thus Christ is a cosmic power leading his followers to the realms of light where he will reign in glory. For Bultmann the Cross and Resurrection are a "cosmic unity" and an "eschatological event." Cf. *Kerygma und Mythos* (1948), I, p. 49.; G. Quispel in F. L. Cross (Ed.), *The Jung Codex* (1955), p. 76 seq.

44. Rom. 5:14.

45. Its most familiar modern form is Freemasonry, in which emphasis is laid upon secret, or at least restricted, knowledge acquired through progressive initiation into the cult. For a popular exposition of Masonic rituals and tenets *vide* Walton Hannah, *Darkness Visible* (1952).

SELECT BIBLIOGRAPHY

(of works not mentioned previously)

Barclay, W.   *Letters to the Seven Churches*, 1957.
Barnes, A. S.   *The Martyrdom of St. Peter and St. Paul*, 1933.
Barrett, C. K.   *Luke the Historian in Recent Study*, 1961.
Bevan, G. M.   *Early Christians of Rome, their Words and Pictures*, 1927.
Case, S. J.   *Jesus, A New Biography*, 1927.
Crowfoot, J. W.   *Early Churches in Palestine*, 1941.
Dalman, G.   *Sacred Sites and Ways*, 1935.
Davies, W. D.   *Christian Origins and Judaism*, 1962.
Doresse, J.   *Les livres secrets des gnostiques d'Égypte*, 1958.
                     L'Évangile selon Thomas, 1959.
Duncan, J. G.   *Digging up Biblical History*, 1931. 2 Vols.
Elder, J.   *Archaeology and the Bible*, 1960.
Frothingham, A. L.   *The Monuments of Christian Rome*, 1908.
Glueck, N.   *The River Jordan*, 1946.
Harding, G. L.   *The Antiquities of Jordan*, 1959.
Hollis, F. J.   *The Archaeology of Herod's Temple*, 1934.
Ilton, P.   *Digging in the Holy Land*, 1959.
Jeremias, J.   *Unknown Sayings of Jesus*, 1957.
Kahle, P.   *The Cairo Genizah*, 1947.
Kirschbaum, E.   *The Tombs of St. Peter and St. Paul*, 1959.
Lanciani, R.   *Ancient and Modern Rome*, 1925.
Lowrie, W.   *Monuments of the Early Church*, 1901.
                     SS. Peter and Paul in Rome, 1940.
Mackinnon, A. G.   *The Rome of Saint Paul*, 1930.
                     The Rome of the Early Church, 1933.

Milik, J. T.   *Ten Years of Discovery in the Wilderness of Judaea*, 1959.

Moulton, J. H.   *From Egyptian Rubbish Heaps*, 1916.
Muir, J.   *The Spade and the Scriptures*, 1940.
Owen, G. F.   *Archaeology and the Bible*, 1961.
Perowne, S.   *The Life and Times of Herod the Great*, 1956.
Peters, J. P.   *Bible and Spade*, 1923.
Riddle, D. W.   *Paul, Man of Conflict*, 1940.
Schonfield, H. J.   *The Bible Was Right*, 1959.
Schubert, K.   *The Dead Sea Community*, 1959.
Stonehouse, N. B.   *Paul Before the Areopagus*, 1949.
Sutcliffe, E. F.   *The Monks of Qumran*, 1960.
Thompson, J. A.   *Archaeology and the Bible*, 1962.
van Unnik, W. C.   *Newly Discovered Gnostic Writings*, 1960.
Wilson, R. McL.   *The Gospel of Philip*, 1963.
Wiseman, D. J.   *Illustrations From Biblical Archaeology*, 1959.

Wright, G. E. and
  Freedman, D. N.   *The Biblical Archaeologist Reader*, 1961.

INDEX

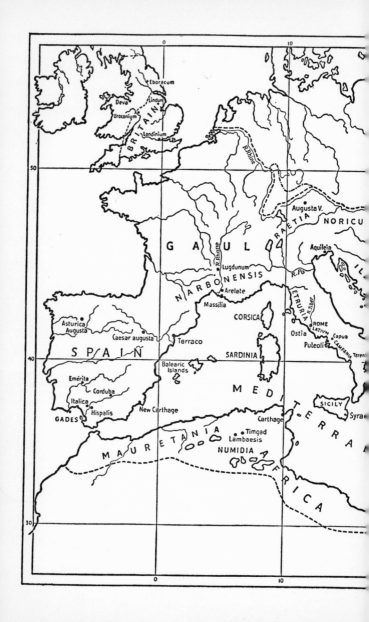

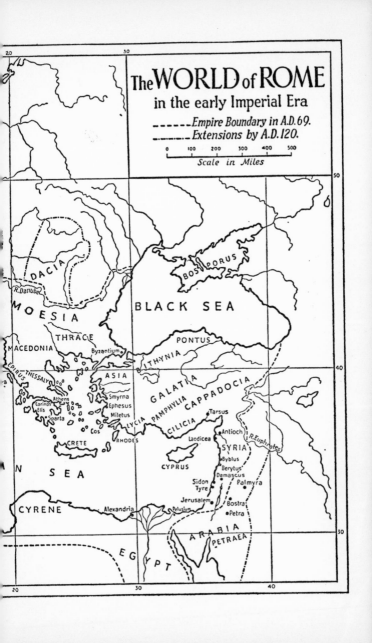

The WORLD of ROME
in the early Imperial Era

------- Empire Boundary in A.D. 69.
── ── Extensions by A.D.120.

0 100 200 300 400 500
Scale in Miles

DACIA

R.Danube

MOESIA

THRACE

MACEDONIA

EPIRUS

THESSALY

Byzantium

BITHYNIA

ASIA

Athens
Corinth
Elis
Sparta

Smyrna
Ephesus
Miletus

Cos

RHODES

CRETE

BLACK SEA

BOSPORUS

PONTUS

GALATIA

CAPPADOCIA

LYCIA PAMPHYLIA

CILICIA

Tarsus

Antioch

R.Euphrates

Laodicea

CYPRUS

SYRIA

Byblus
Berytus
Damascus
Palmyra

Sidon
Tyre

Jerusalem

Bostra

Petra

N SEA

CYRENE

Alexandria

Pelusium

EGYPT

ARABIA

PETRAEA